GW01230170

10 Steps To Finding Mr. "Not-So" Perfect

By:
Patricia Kennedy Louke

Copyright 2024 by Patricia Kennedy Louke All rights reserved.

No portion of this book may be reproduced in any form without written permission from the publisher or author, except as permitted by U.S. copyright law.

Dedication

Dedicated to Charley:

My Mr. "Not-So" Perfect who became Mr. Perfect for me.

Table of Contents

Prologue 1

Step 1 Location, Location, Location 7

Step 2 A Picture Is Worth A Few Words 32

Step 3 Safety First 43

Step 4 Grocery List 56

Step 5 Swipe Right, Swipe Left 69

Step 6 Kindergarten 77

Step 7 Three Strikes Before You're Out 85

Step 8 Sabotage 93

Step 9 Dating Fatigue 106

Step 10 The Dating Dance 115

Conclusion: 132

Prologue

Dating at any age takes a lot of courage.

Whether you are new to dating or re-entering the dating world, it can be uncomfortable exploring new encounters. There is a level of vulnerability everyone will experience; you are not alone. Think of dating as a journey. A journey involves moving from one place to another. A journey can be an adventurous and exciting journey or a self-discovering and introspective journey. Your dating journey may incorporate both, leading to moments of adventure followed by moments of self-discovery. While on any journey, keep your sense of humor, take things in stride, and enjoy yourself. Admittedly, you cannot always be in control of everything that happens during a journey; however, ideally you are in control of your destiny.

When you reminisce about a trip you have taken in the past, it is usually an unexpected event, a catastrophic, or funny situation that brings a smile to your face. These same types of surprises may happen while you search for a match. Although it may not seem funny at the time, when you look back on the situation, it can make you laugh. If all else fails, it turns into a good story to share with your friends.

Try to set realistic expectations for yourself. Finding your match usually does not happen overnight. Like any journey or trip, it requires planning, preparation, active participation, and effort. This book is a guide to help you navigate the intricacies of the dating world, making your journey easier and more enjoyable. Congratulations on taking the first steps on your brave new journey.

The title, "Mr. "Not-So" Perfect" reminds us that no one is perfect. The "Prince Charming" of your dreams may have a few flaws, or not look exactly like you pictured. It should be noted that there is no algorithm or a specific number of frogs you have to kiss before finding your prince. Some people meet their match on their very first date. I actually know someone this happened to. Surprisingly, one date is all it took, and they currently remain happily married. Fairy tales can come true in the real world.

On the other hand, people like me take a bit longer and require a lot more exertion before they find their matches.

Your match may be found in a face-to-face encounter or the digital world. We will look at these options in Step 1. Wherever you may find your match, engaging conversation is necessary for a successful encounter. Conversational skills are important, allowing a sense of belonging, decreasing loneliness, and increasing your social charisma. Starting a conversation with someone you do not know should be a college course. The art of talking has been replaced with texting and emails, predominantly among the younger generation, although it did not take long for the older generation to catch on. When starting a conversation, be positive, which includes your body language, so smile and make eye contact. Let's look at some ways to start a conversation, so you can start practicing your conversation skills today.

Ask a question. The question can be related to your surroundings. If at an eatery, you can ask what he recommends on the menu or what he is having for lunch. While you're enjoying the outdoors, you can ask about the weather or whatever outdoor activity you are currently engaged in. If you're currently attending a workshop, ask about the speaker or the topic of discussion. Whatever the question, attentively listen to the response, then formulate another question to keep the conversation moving forward. Open-ended questions will elicit a deeper response. An example of an open-ended question might be, "Have you been to other productions at this playhouse?" You then can discuss the various plays you both have attended. This type of question requires a person to share their experiences with you.

Pay a compliment. Everyone likes compliments. An example is to simply say: That is a nice jacket, briefcase, or car. Promptly following your compliment, ask a question regarding the item you just complimented. It is all right to embellish a little by saying you are looking for a similar gift for your brother's upcoming birthday, or you are currently car shopping. You can always confess later that you were just trying to engage him in conversation.

Discussing current events is easy as long as you stay away from politics and religion. I suggest trying pop culture events as an alternative. For instance, "Did you see the latest Tik-Tok challenge or the latest popular movie?" Alternatively, "Do you like an iPhone versus an Android? I am thinking about getting a new cell phone and am trying to decide if I should switch brands."

Asking for help will elicit a response and open conversational opportunities. We all need assistance with everything from home repairs, gardening advice, obtaining directions, or carrying a heavy item. People in general like to share their knowledge and are rewarded with a sense of pride when helping others. If it does not go against your moral code, play a little damsel in distress. Princess Leia from Star Wars is a strong female who started as a damsel in distress (needing a man's assistance) but still managed to develop a powerful role. In contrast to asking for help, offer to help an individual. Offering your assistance is usually welcomed if you are knowledgeable on the subject matter, or if you genuinely want to participate in the activity.

Being straightforward and introducing yourself is a bold but rewarding action. Explain that you are new to the event, area, or activity and want to say hello. Ask a leading question such as: "Can you recommend where to find the best pizza?" or "Can you give me some advice about (whatever's happening)?"

Initiate a conversation and see if it picks up momentum. Undoubtedly, you will know if your conversation naturally flows or comes to a screeching halt. If it comes to a halt, just thank this person for their time and go about the rest of your day. Use this encounter as a practice attempt and know you will find another person to hone your new skills with soon.

Everyday life and encounters are opportunities to meet someone and practice your conversation skills. The grocery store's frozen food section was always popular; however, these days you are more likely to meet someone in the ready-made meal line after work. Instead of having DoorDash deliver your meal, get dressed, and go out to the store. As a result, you may find someone else picking up a meal for one. Picking up your dry cleaning, a bottle of wine, a lottery ticket, or anywhere you are waiting in line is an opportunity to engage with another person.

Begin practicing your conversational skills with different people, regardless of their age or sex. After you are comfortable initiating a conversation, try your skills on a person you might like to date. Most importantly, don't forget to have fun! If you are having fun, so will the people you meet.

Now, let's delve into the 10 Steps to finding your Mr. "Not-So" Perfect!

Step 1
Location, Location, Location

Location, location, location is the number one rule in real estate. This means identical homes can vary greatly in availability and value depending solely on the location. A similar logic can be applied to dating when it comes to finding your match.

So where is Mr. "Not-So" Perfect located? Are you looking in the right geographical location? Are you looking at face-to-face encounters or the digital world? The answer might be to look at each section and see what works best for you.

Geographical location:

Where you explore dating is very subjective: your personal preferences will lead you toward various physical locations. These locations are usually based on your driving circumference for work and leisure activities. In the event these locations do not yield a positive result, it is then time to challenge yourself to expand your geographic area.

For instance, are you open to relocating? The average American moves 11.7 times in their lifetime. (I am not sure how you move a 0.7th of a time, but that is the current statistic.) If you always wanted to live in the city, perhaps this is a good time to look at that location. Meeting someone in a new location can help with the transition. Even if this person does not turn out to be your Mr. Perfect, he could turn out to be a good friend who helps you navigate your new locale.

The majority of people would like to meet someone in their backyard and are not interested in entertaining any form of relocation. One-third of the population never leaves the town where they grew up, and as a result, these people have very limited interactions. Your backyard may be a good place to begin looking for your match, but not the only place to explore. Dorothy from "The Wizard of Oz" said, "There is no place like home," but Dorothy went on one huge adventure, and if she had airplanes versus a hot air balloon, she might have lived very happily in the Land of Oz. Your match's location may pleasantly surprise you by offering you a new utopia or Land of Oz.

Geographical location with online dating will be discussed later; for now, make an effort to broaden your horizons by trying different geographical areas. I am not saying to take a trip to France (although that would be nice), but simply explore new towns or places while taking some day trips to destinations that interest you.

One last thought about meeting someone outside of your geographically desired area is that perhaps your match is willing to relocate to your area. Unless this match is located in a different state, this is not a question for the first date. Your goal is not to scare him away, but this possibility is something you should not rule out. If all the stars align, and you are both in love, you will find a way to make the rest work, including a location where you both will be happy.

Face-to-face locations:

With face-to-face encounters, you can get an accurate picture of how someone looks, carries themselves, their energy level, and overall personality. By implementing a few of the suggestions below, you are engaging in live human contact, using all of your senses. There are a multitude of opportunities available allowing for a face-to-face encounter.

Join a tour group while on vacation or a day trip. If you are staying close to home, become a local tourist. I have attended local tours of my town's downtown alone and with friends. Not only can you meet an interesting group of people: you can also enjoy the bonus of learning the local culture. Historical tours are often run by local museums, women's clubs, or local entrepreneurs. Free walking tours (usually tip-based) offer engaging and eclectic adventures. Free walking tours allow you to schedule a tour and afterward pay your tour guide what you feel it is worth. Of course, they do have a suggested donation. I have attended several of these free walking tours in various locations, domestic and abroad, and am happy to report I have never been disappointed. Google "free walking tours" in your desired location and see what comes up.

Another entertaining activity is participating in scavenger hunts, which have become very popular and are an enjoyable way to meet people. A scavenger hunt is a game where participants gather specific items on a list, usually without purchasing them. During a scavenger hunt, you will work in small teams while competing against other teams for a prize. Scavenger hunts may be organized by a local charity, town organization or, due to their popularity, are now offered by tour companies.

Regardless of the location, it is imperative to be approachable and observant of your surroundings. Perhaps you are missing opportunities to engage in conversations because you are closed off, busy, or distracted with other thoughts, consequently missing out on meeting a potential match. People frequently pull out their cell phones when alone in a public place, which does not invite conversation from another individual. Instead of pulling out your cell phone, take out the earbuds, and look around you. It may feel awkward or uncomfortable at first but stay with it. Make an art out of people watching. Your goal while people-watching is not to be unobtrusive; on the contrary, it is to be open to conversation. For example, when at an eatery, try removing the extra place setting. This will let people know you are not expecting anyone and indicate your availability. Having a book or prop with you will provide someone an opportunity to ask you an opening question, but if you are actively reading this book without eye contact, then you are again closed off.

Encounters can happen when you least expect them. A neighbor met her husband while sitting next to him on an airplane. I missed an opportunity on an elevator ride at work once, or so my colleague told me, since I was unaware this person was flirting with me. Remain open and aware while allowing others to speak with you, or go that extra step and start a conversation with them.

Parks are great local places to run into people on a beautiful day. Here you can find an array of activities, from enjoying a leisurely walk, taking in the views while sitting on a park bench, or observing a baseball game (preferably the adult male teams). Seriously, look at your town's adult male sporting events and casually stop by.

Do not forget our furry friends for an outing at your area dog parks. By simply changing the times, days, and location of your doggy outings, you will increase your interactions with different people. People tend to be creatures of habit, falling into a routine, even as simple as going to a dog park on a particular day and time. With this in mind, if you meet a person of interest, be sure to ask if this is their regular time for their doggy outing and encourage another play date. Another great place to bring your dog is Yappy Hour, where pet-friendly venues offer special deals for dog owners, such as discounted drinks or treats for humans and their pets, and periodically amusing contests with prizes. Even during your routine dog walk, try taking different routes. You never know whose path you may cross while seeing some different scenery. Your pet is an important part of your life, so naturally you would like your match to be pet-friendly.

If you don't have a pet of your own, offer to walk your friends' or neighbors' dog. I had a neighbor with a fun-loving boxer named Dexter, who needed a walk at lunchtime. I worked from home, so walking Dexter forced me to take a break from the computer and get some fresh air. Having never owned a dog, I was pleasantly surprised at the welcoming community of animal lovers. On every walk, interactions with other people were guaranteed. Maybe it was Dexter's amazing Frisbee catching that wowed the people. Your pet makes a great wingman, providing numerous opportunities to meet someone, so be sure to include your pet on some fun outings.

Let's revisit the supermarket. A new Spanish social media trend is encouraging people to find romantic prospects in supermarkets. The phenomenon, known as "Pineapple-gate" claims that singles can find love by placing an upside-down pineapple in their shopping cart when shopping between 7pm-8pm. I am not sure if this has trended in the US, but if you are purchasing a pineapple you might wish to place it upside down in your cart. Re-double your efforts by holding an upside-down pineapple while waiting in the meals to go line!

Volunteering for a charitable event or charity is a wonderful way to get involved in your community while giving back. You can volunteer for a specific favorite charity, or you can choose an event and see if they need additional volunteers. These activities will help connect you to people who share your values while offering many different ways to contribute. Every event needs a host of volunteers to organize and run the event. I have found that participating as a volunteer on the day of the event is always rewarding and enjoyable. One of my favorite events was volunteering for a casino night. Whatever you participate in, there is usually a post- volunteer gathering as a thank-you for all the volunteers, which is another opportunity to meet someone. Ongoing volunteer opportunities include dog walking for animal shelters, serving at soup kitchens, and being a docent at museums, just to name a few. You can offer to assist with a set number of hours weekly or monthly. To find out who needs help, you only need to ask.

Festivals and concerts are a great place to meet someone, typically offering an immediate common interest. Free summer outdoor concerts are offered by many municipalities, so grab a lawn chair and enjoy some music. Music is such a powerful tool for bringing people together while providing ample opportunities to connect in song, dance, or simple conversation. Festivals are predominantly theme-based. Find a festival that speaks to you. For instance, are you interested in films, culture, or food festivals? There are many different types of festivals for you to choose from, with just as many different formats, including classes, demonstrations, vendors, speakers, educational interactions, food, and/or music.

Bookstores do more than just sell books and are open to all. Most bookstores offer an author event, which can include a discussion, book reading, book signings, and a pre- or post-event event social hour. Our local bookstore offers Cinema and Conversation once a month, a free event where you watch a movie and have a discussion afterward. Various types of book clubs that can be found at your bookstore are usually distinguished by either the topic or by gender. Libraries are another wonderful place for finding book clubs, speakers on various topics, and even board game nights all geared toward adult gatherings. To sum this up, even if you are not a "reader," check out your local bookstore or library for a wide array of adult events.

Independent coffee shops have morphed into the cooler version of a bookstore or library. On any given day, you will find people at a coffee shop socializing. The trendier coffee shops have board games set up to play, special events like trivia night, a local musician performance, or poetry readings. This type of meeting place encourages people to stay and intermingle with others. See which coffee shops are hosting events in your area while grabbing your cup of coffee.

Expand your horizons by taking a class or two. High school adult education classes are very reasonably priced and; for the most part, offer "fun" classes since no college credits are involved. If you've always wanted to learn another language or musical instrument, grab your adult education pamphlet and give it a try. If cooking is more of an interest, many grocery stores offer cooking classes, as do some local restaurants and culinary stores. These cooking classes are for all skill levels, so don't worry if cooking is not your forte. You can enjoy the creative side of preparing a fabulous meal followed by the indulgence of consuming your delectable creations; all topped off with a pairing of wine. Perhaps there is an artist inside of you clamoring to escape. A painting or pottery class can offer this opportunity. Art classes are very welcoming and relaxing, and often, you can find these at your local art galleries or art museums. Practical classes such as those offered by Home Depot and Lowes appeal to men who want to learn home improvement skills.

These stores offer a wide range of DIY projects covering indoor and outdoor topics relevant to everyone. Check your local store for dates, times, and types of projects currently being offered. Ultimately, you will find a class that resonates with you. Gyms offer a wide variety of classes with the added benefit of improving your health, and in the end, you will feel and look better for your participation. Prefer to be outdoors? Try yoga or tai chi in the park or on the beach; both are popular among men and women. Many health fitness classes offer a "drop-in" or one-time rate, so you can sample the class without purchasing a full membership, a win-win situation.

Don't forget college classes. Many adults are returning to college for a career change or to assist with career advancement. Tuition reimbursement is a benefit offered by many employers, allowing an affordable means to take advantage of this opportunity. For seniors, many states have a program allowing senior citizens to take free college courses. Generally, these are offered as low as age 55; however, the exact age depends upon the state. When taking a college course, attending in person is ideal since online courses will have limited interaction with other people. In addition, sign up for a study group if one is offered. As a rule, not only will a study group help with the course, but you will also meet new people and broaden your social circle.

Getting involved at work, like going to the gym, is another win-win situation. This will demonstrate initiative to your managers while bolstering your annual review or performance plan. Achieve this by joining a team or committee that helps further your career growth, namely training sessions, workshops, or career development sessions. Many companies conduct charitable work events, which provide another avenue for work participation and growth. Involving yourself in any of these work activities expands your colleague interactions while enhancing your career. One word of caution: whenever getting involved at work, only speak positively about work and your other work colleagues. Negative comments will reflect poorly on you, undoing all of your good efforts.

Friends, relatives, and neighbors are another wonderful and overlooked resource. Let people know you are interested in meeting someone, even people like your dental hygienist and sister-in-law's mother. In other words, networking is the key to promoting yourself. My niece is dating someone her hairdresser introduced her to, and all things are pointing toward a future engagement announcement.

Kevin Bacon says there are six degrees of separation, meaning any two people on earth can be linked together through six or fewer acquaintances. You need to spread the word and ask your family and friends to spread the word. Get the word out any way you can (short of taking out a billboard advertisement along the highway)!

Bars, clubs, or pubs are tough since locality and alcohol are the main commonality. These locations have worked for some, particularly if it is a neighborhood place where "everyone knows your name". If everyone does not know your name, there should be someone who can vouch for the person you just met.

Alcohol can impede your judgment, so please do not leave with someone you do not know. Exchange contact information and leave with the friend you came out with. If you are going to an establishment to dance and/or hopefully meet someone, go with one friend. It is intimidating for a man to approach a group of females, attempting to single you out. If you are with a group of friends, you may have to make the first move. A little eye contact and a friendly smile can go a long way. Simply hold your eye contact for three seconds, letting him know you are interested, then glance away. Next look back to see if he is acknowledging you. Once you receive an acknowledgment, smile again with a little nod of your head, inviting him over. Another approach in these types of social gatherings is to have a friend intercede on your behalf. If you have an outgoing friend who interacts easily, they are a great resource for starting conversations and finding out information on someone you might be interested in. I had a married friend who made it her mission to "interview" potential prospects for us single friends. The information she acquired was entertaining, if nothing else!

There are political organizations or houses of worship venues to explore. These groups will narrow your interactions to like-minded beliefs. If staying within a particular religion or political party is important to you, these venues offer a safe space. Some religions even offer single mixers to encourage matches within their beliefs. Both venues have various ways of getting involved at your local level.

One of the best places to look for a match is while engaging in an activity you enjoy. If you do something you enjoy, you will meet people with similar interests while having a good time. On the other hand, even if you do not meet a match, you are still enjoying the activity. You can find clubs or groups for almost any imaginable activity. A new club forming across the US is called Silent Reading, where you meet at a particular time, read your individual book quietly, and then have a social hour to discuss the reading. A good place to look for clubs and activities is in your local newspaper or online under community events.

Meet-up.com is another excellent online resource and a popular favorite. With Meet-up, you simply enter your location and view activities currently being offered. All activities are organized by individuals like you. These activities are usually held in a public location. The time and date will depend on which activity you choose. On this site, if you do not see what you are looking for, you can start a group with a few simple steps. Groups can range from archery to wine tasting and everything in between. When choosing a club, favor one that includes both men and women, if your objective is to meet a man. If you are simply looking to widen your social circle, go for anything that brings a smile to your face.

Professional groups are a good way to meet people with similar career goals. There are several young professional groups, small business groups, your chamber of commerce, and entrepreneurial organizations to choose from. In addition, there are groups for specific professions, like the American Accounting Association. Searching for a professional group, either broad-based or specific, will yield many results from your local level to the national level.

An area to explore which is quite often overlooked is your past. Reconnecting with a past relationship is now easy via the internet. That old high school heartthrob or the one that got away in college could be there waiting for you to reconnect. Why wait for a reunion when you can use LinkedIn, Facebook, Instagram, and other social media apps including Google searches to help with these re-connections? LinkedIn is a social platform that people use to build and engage their professional business network; Facebook and Instagram focus more on members' personal lives. A general Google search is simply opening the Google search engine and typing in a name along with any contact information you might have, such as an address, phone number, birthday, current city, or year of high school graduation. My friend married someone she reconnected with from her past, and they recently happily celebrated their first anniversary.

Singles groups offer a more focused target. There

is a wide variety of single groups, including speed dating, parents without partners, singles travel, singles dances, parties, and mixers, just to name a few. There is even a singles event where you bring your dog with you, who (as previously discussed) is a great partner in crime. The in-person single mixers are becoming very popular again, especially with 18 – 29-year-olds who are experiencing dating app fatigue. Dating experts say the in-person events are a great chance to get off your phone and meet people who may shine better in person. Matchmakers or paid dating services are another option currently in vogue, particularly for those with demanding work schedules. These can be quite expensive, so be sure to thoroughly investigate what you are purchasing. Here you enter into a contract with a service provided for a set fee. In return, the service provider is offering you a specific number of dates over a particular time. These dates are supposed to meet your dating criteria. A word of advice here: specify your detailed dating criteria in the contract. The contract should also contain detailed clauses in the event the service provider does not deliver the specific number of dates in your specified time frame. I recommend reviewing any service provider on the Better Business Bureau website or on another third-party website for customer satisfaction and success rate.

Given all of the above suggestions on locations to explore, the key takeaway is to broaden your social circle. Even if you do not meet someone, you are expanding your horizons while fostering personal growth. Making friends of any sex will enrich your life, and who knows? They may have a brother, friend, or cousin who would be perfect for you. Odds are Mr. "Not-So" Perfect will not walk up and knock on your door without a little help.

Trends come and go, even with finding a match. The graph below by Anderson shows the timeframe from 2009 to 2017 where people are meeting each other. With the digital world becoming our focus, we have forgotten to engage people in our quests. Notice that meeting someone through family, friends, and neighbors has dramatically declined. I feel these are missed opportunities. Remember that people like to help others. As I've said previously, there is something very satisfying about making another person happy. Reaching out to others does make us vulnerable, but the results can be very fulfilling. Let these people who care about you give you a helping hand, given that they do have your best interests at heart. If they do not personally know someone, ask them for advice on where to meet someone. They may have the perfect suggestion and one we have not thought of.

How heterosexual couples have met, data from 2009 and 2017

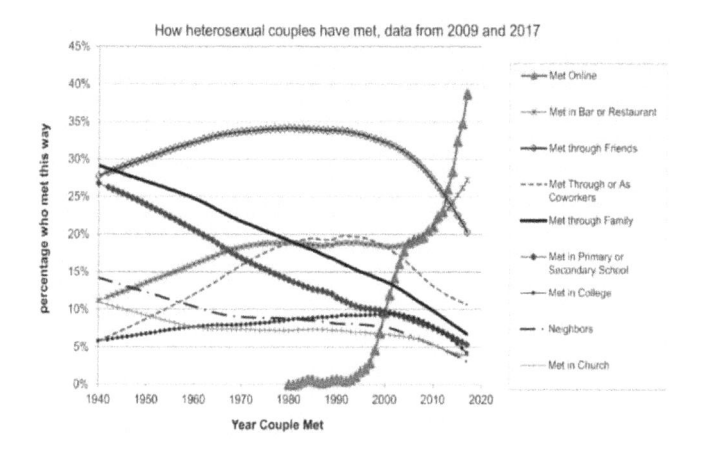

Online dating:

Let's look at the elephant in the room: online dating. Currently, 70% of those using online dating have led to an exclusive relationship for 18 – 29-year-olds. However, online dating is not just for the younger generation. Note that 40% of all age singles say they have tried a dating app, and this percentage increases every year.

There are sites for every type of relationship and every age group. Society has given its blessing to online dating because this format has resulted in the successful matching of numerous people. Online dating has widened dating options, giving birth to a new method of locating your significant other. In a nutshell, these people's paths would not have crossed any other way, making online dating the predominant way people currently meet. The staggering statistic that supports online dating is that one-third of all married people today have met online. However, that still leaves two-thirds of people meeting their spouses in real-time, many through the in-person methods we previously discussed.

There is a present-day shift with 18 – 29-year-olds to meet in person again, as mentioned previously. I hope this trend continues, since isolating behind a computer screen reduces social skills. However, it is currently not enough to register on the Richter scale or to affect the mass appeal of dating apps. Online dating is here to stay and will be a paramount form of intermingling for singles. The question is if online dating is right for you.

People were asked if meeting in-person or meeting online had a positive or negative effect on the relationship. The results were inconsequential. 50% of the online daters felt neither positive nor negative. 54% of the in-person daters said it was just as successful. So, it is a personal preference on how you wish to date. For this reason, I suggest you do not limit yourself to one avenue of dating.

Enter the online dating world, but do not stop trying the in-person approaches, especially since there are so many options to choose from.

Have you ever wondered why online dating is so popular? The simple answer is most people have a computer, so there is easy access for a lot of singles. You can do the preliminary work in the comfort of your own home, at your convenience, while in your pajamas. When you do get to the stage of meeting someone in person, you are going out with the specific purpose of meeting an individual. This person has already expressed interest in meeting you, therefore removing a major portion of the guesswork, such as whether he is available or in a relationship. Like everything in life, there are pluses and minuses to online dating, which we will look at later. Right now, let's look at this fresh commodity.

Upon entering the world of online dating for the first time, you may feel overwhelmed, understandably, since it is estimated there are 2,500 different online dating apps in the US. Even Facebook has entered the online dating world. Which site to choose may become your first hurdle to overcome. I suggest you "ask like-minded friends" where they have had success, and then look at several sites for your comfort level. You may like the format or aesthetics of one site versus another. Your geographical location may lead you to a specific site, given that different sites are more popular in different geographical areas. For example, the site Plenty of Fish in one state could suggest a casual hookup; yet in another state, it turned out to be the most popular site among the over-40-year-old age group. Different sites will also appeal to different age groups. For instance, Bumble appeals to younger ages versus Silver Seniors to older ages. Reality television shows have made dating a farmer or dating a cowboy a possibility, allowing these niche lifestyles their specific dating platforms. You can Google which sites are best for your age and the type of relationship you are seeking, starting you down the right path.

Choosing a free dating site versus a fee-based dating site is another consideration. There is some belief that people who pay a fee are more serious or committed to finding their match since they have a financial investment. While there may be some truth to this, I still suggest starting with a free dating site. A free dating site is a good way to see if you even like this type of interaction, because we know online dating is not for everyone. A free site allows you the time to navigate your course and to try some different approaches within your profile. You can relax and see if your profile's verbiage or photos attract the type of person you are seeking without feeling like you are paying for this time. In other words, take your time and perfect your profile, tweaking it until you feel it represents the best you.

In my opinion, timing is the most important element and not necessarily fee- based versus a free dating site. I had a fee-based dating site tell me I was "unmatchable." Even though this fee-based dating site did not have any matches for me, they did not refund my money. I am confident that my criteria were not so strict to be declared unmatchable! I recently read this site is being sued by another individual who was also labeled "unmatchable." This article allowed me to feel vindicated, since I was not the only person who encountered this situation. However, I still lost the financial investment, not to mention the time, aggravation, and damage to my self-esteem. Eventually, I met my Mr. "Not-So" Perfect on a free site, which, frankly, surprised me. I was one of those people among the mindset that fee-based dating sites held more serious-minded individuals. I tried the free dating site with a "what the heck" attitude and ended up admitting once again I was wrong to judge.

Once you have picked an online dating site that suits you, the first step is to create your profile. Some dating sites ask for a profile headline, which is a short one-line phrase summarizing your personality or interest. A headline can run the gamut from funny to serious or intriguing to straightforward. These can also reference a particular activity or hobby. Whichever description fits you; everyone agrees it needs to be catchy. If you need a little assistance, there are several articles online with a list of headline phrases, so finding one that fits your personality should not prove to be too difficult. Some examples of headlines are: "Willing to lie about how we met," "Let's be each other's reason for getting off this dating site," or "When life brings you lemons, sprinkle them over oysters and invite everyone over for supper." If you are not finding the perfect headline for you, proceed to the main verbiage of your profile. Once you have figured out how to present yourself, the perfect headline may create itself.

The main verbiage or biography of your profile is where you introduce yourself and tell a little bit about what you do and like to do, in addition to briefly describing what you are looking for. Here are some beneficial tips for creating your biography:

- ❖ Be honest and authentic.
- ❖ Keep it short and sweet, no essays.
- ❖ Tell people what type of relationship you are seeking. I do not propose looking for marriage

only. A better term might be "seeking a long-term commitment."

❖ Use action words like adventurous, outgoing, and artistic. Pick three that describe you.

❖ State your interests or hobbies, something that the person you are seeking would also be interested in. Not many men wish to share arts and crafts with you. Museums or hiking might be a better choice if these are things you like.

❖ A funny situation or weird event can help you stand out from the crowd.

❖ Asking a question can start a line of communication. An example might be: I love to read. Can you recommend a good book?

The goal of your profile is to start a conversation. With this in mind, use your best sales approach. Yes, you are selling yourself and looking for a hook to reel someone in. Once you have reeled someone in, you can decide if you keep him or gently place him back in the pond.

Step 2
A Picture Is Worth A Few Words

Like it or not, men are visual creatures. It takes one-tenth of a second for someone to look at your photo and form a first impression. Online dating does not allow body language, facial expressions, or your personality to shine through. As a result, your photos are even more vital to a successful profile. The goal of your main or primary photo is to engage the viewer, enticing him to look at the other photos you have posted and take the time to read your profile.

When selecting your primary photo for posting, think about how you wish to be portrayed. A sexy photo is fine if you are looking for sex. In this case, you will probably not need in-depth verbiage. A professional headshot shows your business side; however, you are not interviewing for a career. A photo in an expensive outfit while wearing expensive jewelry may leave a man wondering if he can afford your tastes and interests. Portraying a high-maintenance lifestyle will limit your viewing audience.

When creating that first primary headshot photo,

take some professional photography advice. It is essential to make eye contact with the camera. Women should make a flirty face, a wide smile, and/or laugh. You are trying to capture that twinkle in your eyes because your eyes are the windows to the soul, letting your light shine through. Authentic lighting is fundamental when taking a nice photo; therefore, natural light is the most flattering, which is easily achieved by taking outdoor pictures. You should also stick with a simple background by removing eye-wandering distractions and sensory overload in your photos. Avoid a selfie if at all possible; they usually cast an unusual angle on your facial features. Elongate your neck and push your chin forward. It may feel a little awkward, but this position will highlight your features in the most positive manner.

According to Psychology Today, a woman wearing bright-colored clothing will elicit more responses from men. The largest difference was between women who wore red at 6.1% versus black at 4%. Wear something that makes you feel like a million dollars, allowing your self-confidence to shine through your photo. It truly is all about your attitude. A man likes a woman who exemplifies self-confidence. Add a twinkle in your eyes, topped off with a smile, and you have an irresistible photo.

Now that you have an amazing primary headshot photo, you need to assemble your montage. Do not only post one photo, as this will send the wrong message to your viewers. You will appear unmotivated, or not willing to fully invest in the process; therefore, you are not seriously seeking a relationship. One photo will also leave a viewer feeling like you are hiding or embarrassed by something, or that this one photo is not a picture of you at all, but a fake. Take the time to create a worthy profile which needs to include several photos.

The second photo someone wishes to see is a full head-to-toe picture. This second photo is non-negotiable. Without this full-body photo, you are hiding the authentic genuine person you are. Your full body photo is a chance to flaunt your attributes. For instance, do you have long legs, toned arms, or nice curves? If so, highlight these in your pictures. Certain attributes should be kept to a minimum including cleavage. (Recognize that a little mystery is intriguing.) Women tend to obsess about their weight and may therefore avoid the full-body photo. Do not put off that full-body photo until you lose those extra five pounds. Only you will think that five pounds will make a difference. Trust me, it does not. Revisit photo tips for how to take a slimming photo if this is a concern. Men will usually not respond to a profile that does not have a full body photo. Own who you are, and let that self-assurance shine through. You are beautiful just the way you are.

The next several pictures you post will encompass different aspects of your personality, background, and interests. These photos will give your match a peek at who you are. You will want to post four to five photos in total.

Your third photo should be an activity or lifestyle photo. Activity photos are conversation starters that prompt the person to ask you a question. Activities could be attending an event, like a sporting event or concert, participating in an event, like running a marathon or cooking a meal. Another alternative is to just don your favorite team's jersey. Vacation photos also invite conversation, but steer clear of bathing suit photos, which can be overly sexual and inadvertently send the wrong message.

Your fourth and fifth photos might include a dressed-up or dressed-down photo (whichever is currently missing) and a silly fun photo. These remaining photos should give viewers a peek at your whimsical side.

Under no circumstances post photos with other people. This includes group shots, blacking out of others' faces, blurry shots, photos with a friend, photos with children or grandchildren, and especially photos with a man, even if it is your brother. The focus should be on you, so post photos of only you.

Gathering your photos should not be painful. Invite a friend to conduct a photo-shoot with you. Make an entertaining day or two out of pretending you are a model, and your friend is your photographer. If you are older, ask your younger family members to help. The younger generation has grown up taking cell phone pictures utilizing all of the latest editing tools, so consider them experts in this field. If you do not have a family member to assist you, look for a high school or college neighbor who would be happy to have fun in return for a gift card or a nice meal. If necessary, you can always hire a photographer, but that can be pricey.

During your photo-op, have your photographer take pictures of you in different settings wearing different outfits. Break out some props like a hat or flower, but no sunglasses. We want to see your beautiful eyes. There are quick tutorials online which can teach you how to take a good photo. These tutorials will show you how to pose, work the angles, and create an eye-catching photo of yourself. Anna Bey has two 13-minute videos on YouTube titled "10 Tricks to ALWAYS Look Good in Pictures." Anna's instructions on posing are very simple lessons. Bach Photography has a 10-minute video on YouTube titled "14 SIMPLE Photography Tips for Breathtaking Portraits." Bach's instructions help you with angles, composition, colors, and various aspects of taking great portraits. I highly endorse trying a few of these suggestions.

Surprisingly, the photo that generated the most conversations for me was on a boat during sunset. My hair was wind-blown, and I was laughing, which gave me squinty eyes. I thought this was a horrible photo. Yet horrible seeming photos might be just the ticket if they reveal the real you. It showed me with my guard down, just having fun, which in turn invited others to have fun with me. It was also an activity photo that prompted people to ask me questions like, "Do you like boating?" or "Was this taken locally or on vacation?" It turned out to be a great conversation starter and the photo that ignited the most responses.

Unsure which photo represents you the best? Test your photo on Photofeeler. Photofeeler tells you how you are coming across in your pictures. Your photos will go out to a group of people, and you will see which one the group finds most appealing. This way, you use the most advantageous photos in your profile. The service is free if you actively participate by voting on other people's pictures. In other words, you are asking for your photos to be critiqued while critiquing others. If you do not wish to review other pictures, you can purchase credit to have your photos reviewed. On this site, you can set your privacy controls, dictating how long you wish these photos to be reviewed and by whom. You can choose what attributes you wish to be rated, such as whether you look attractive, competent, likable, influential, confident, authentic, fun, smart, trustworthy, and more. These attributes will then be rated on a 1-10 scale. People can also leave you a thoughtful comment on why your photo is being viewed this way. It is surprising how we react to different photos, but even more surprising will be which photo of yours receives the best scores.

Another way to test your photos is to ask a man his opinion. It can be a friend, brother, friend's husband, or just someone of the opposite sex with a different mindset. This man should be in the same demographic you are appealing to. It will not help if you are seeking a 30-year-old man but ask a 60-year-old which photo he prefers.

When I asked my brother his thoughts, he picked a different photo than I had and was quite adamant about his choice. I learned if you ask a man's opinion, do yourself a favor and take his suggestion. Women and men think differently, so profoundly, that a book was written on this very topic. "Men Are From Mars, Women Are From Venus", written by the American relationship counselor John Gray and is still popular over thirty years later. The book states that most common relationship problems between men and women are a result of fundamental psychological differences between the sexes. You can get the summary online and learn the key points in 20 minutes.

Congratulations! You have now picked your four or five best photos based on all of the tips, feedback, and advice. Take one last look at how this collection of photos portrays you. They should tell a little story of who you are while allowing a glimpse into your life. You can always swap out a photo if you create a better one or just want to share a different aspect of yourself. Play around with your photos and have a good time showing different facets of yourself.

Men's photos are a whole different world: remember, men are from Mars! When you are looking at men's photos, do not rule out a bad picture. A large percentage of men do not take the time or painstaking care to post a decent photo, even though they look for a decent photo from a female. Men will not ask for help with taking a photo, so you will see a lot of selfies. Hopefully, the selfie does not involve taking a picture in front of a mirror. Men should take some photo suggestions, but unfortunately, the odds of this happening are not in your favor. There are more females on dating sites than men. 59% of women versus 50% of men have used dating apps. So, the odds are in the men's favor of getting responses even with poor pictures.

Men will post a picture of themselves holding up a fish. Why is this popular? I have no idea, but the fish photos have taken on a life of their own. Gym photos are also popular. While it is nice to see they have a hobby or are into fitness, the photo should be tasteful. You will see photos of men standing with a woman, which, if you are game, offers an opening question by asking them who this woman is. After all, it could be his daughter. Alternatively, perhaps they are subconsciously trying to make you jealous or trying to show you they are dateable and a true catch. Bedroom photos or shirtless photos are the equivalent of overtly sexy photos for women. Once again, if this is your goal, you have found your match. Finally, there are photos without them in it at all, a view of a sunset or favorite pet might actually be showing you their sensitive side. All of these are entertaining and can bring a smile to your face. In the end, you will decide which photo catches your eye, making you pause.

Try to look for the positive when looking at men's online photos. Subtle makeovers are possible further into a relationship, such as a new pair of glasses, a haircut, or an updated wardrobe, are easy to accomplish. Facial hair can be shaved or grown with a little positive encouragement. Those diamonds in the rough can polish up beautifully.

The profiles with poor photos are overlooked quickly by the majority of women. You may wish to rethink this, seeing that these profiles are not getting a lot of attention, so the odds are in your favor for a positive response. If the profile has similar interests, morals, and values, a poor photo should not stop you from exploring further.

I'm a case in point. A couple of my long-term relationships actually started with horrible photos. When I met them in person, I was pleasantly surprised and wished I had dressed a little better or paid more attention to my hair. This includes my Mr. "Not-So" Perfect's online photo, which was blurry and difficult to fully distinguish. Of course, after meeting him and realizing he was handsome, I did not tell him he needed a better photo. That was a secret I kept to myself. Given these points, there are double standards for men versus women with photos, yes. But what else is new?

Step 3
Safety First

Unfortunately, not everyone is honest or trustworthy. This can happen when meeting someone at a social event or on the internet. What makes the internet especially challenging, however, is its additional level of obscurity. You are not seeing someone's body language, hearing their voice, or looking them in the eyes to judge truthfulness. Subsequently, you can communicate with a total fabrication and have no way to verify this until you meet in person. For these reasons, please enter the online dating world with vigilance.

There is a new feature on current cell phones that will allow you to verify a person by just using their photo. You do not need to know any personal information at all. My daughter recently informed me that people are using this feature with online dating to verify the person they are speaking with is not fictitious. This feature is called the Circle to Search. Simply circle the photo of the person you are interested in, and the internet will retrieve all information relating to this photo. The program was actually created to find similar products for shopping. For example: circle a pair of sunglasses in a magazine and locate the stores where these sunglasses can be purchased. Ingenious people quickly applied this to profile pictures. This feature can relay if the person is authentic, resulting in a brilliant safety feature. If your cell phone has the Circle and Search feature, give it a try.

When creating your profile, do not use your full real name. Your profile name can be something eye-catching or a nickname. You can create a profile name that shows your personality like Charming Dimples or Jazzy Lady. Avoid reducing your username to one particular hobby or interest, for example: Scubadiver86. What if the person looking at profiles does not like to scuba dive? Your username says scuba diving is very important to you, which can limit your responses if this is not a shared interest.

Nicknames are always easy to use without being too kitschy. Take a few moments to see what other women have used on the dating site you are considering. If you see first names only, then go with a nickname. If you see adjectives or verbs highlighting interests, then be a little more creative to stand out from the crowd. Stuck? Spin XO is a free username generator. Go to this site and enter some fun facts about you, hit spin, and see what names are generated. If you do not like any of the names, change your entries and try again. This site does not require anything to be downloaded; it's free and is very simple to use, so give it a spin.

It's safer to alter your demographics slightly to protect your identity – specifically, your birthday and geographic location. Your birthday should reflect your actual age or birth year, but you can change the month and/or date. I am aware that many online users alter the year they were born, both men and women, particularly as we get a little older. I have difficulty defending altering your birth year. You are intentionally misleading someone, and eventually, the truth will come to light. I understand why people may alter their age; they feel vibrant, are very active, or look youthful and are seeking the same. However, this can be reflected in the age range you're seeking or mentioned in the verbiage of your profile. Of course, the decision is yours in what birth year you ultimately enter.

The other demographic some people choose to slightly alter is the exact town they live in. You might choose to enter a neighboring town as your location. If your distance circumference includes a major city, but you are not a city person, move your location to a town where the circumference keeps you in the suburbs or vice versa. This will still give you the age range and location range you are seeking without leaving behind your personal information. I am not suggesting altering your location significantly, perhaps five to ten miles, depending on your driving comfort level. An alternative to altering your location is to search for your matches using the zip code of the area you desire. I have used the latter method in an attempt to stay in the suburbs, yielding good results. I lived close to NYC, but the complexity of that commute was a time constraint that I needed to avoid. Searching with a more rural zip code allowed me matches outside of the city. I am told either method works if this is an area of importance for you. Again, you are not trying to be misleading. You are attempting to attract the right person while maintaining safety.

Be leery of profiles that are picture-perfect. I am distrustful of a "model" like photo, especially when there is only one picture. You can always ask for more photos if this profile interests you, but I usually do not put forth the effort or engage at all. Believe in the saying, "If something looks too good to be true, then it usually is." One exception is if you are a model and looking to date another model, then perhaps it is real. Then again, when did a model only post one picture of himself? Something to think about!

If someone tells you they are out of the country, please raise the red flag immediately. This person will eventually ask you for money to get back to the USA or money to visit you. A long-distance relationship of this caliber requires a private jet.

Without any exception never send or give someone money. Everyone initially says they would never fall for this; however, it is amazing how capable and talented some con artists are. You might want to check out the true crime documentary titled, "The Tinder Swindler". The documentary tells the story of an Israeli con man who used Tinder to connect with women. He then emotionally manipulated these women into financially supporting his lavish lifestyle. It is natural to want to believe someone. Women tend to be caring, nurturing, and giving, which can also make us easy targets.

Anyone asking for your personal email address or phone number right away might be trying to hack into your accounts. A typical scam goes something like this: a person says they only have one more day left on the dating site, but would love to meet you. There is not sufficient time to communicate, so please send them your personal contact information so they can communicate with you directly. I say if they want to communicate with you, meet you, and in their heart know you are the one; they will sign up for another month and pay the one-month fee. Do not be fooled by this, regardless of how sincere they sound or how attractive you might find them. The number one crime with online dating is identity theft. Because of this, use the dating site for all communication until after you meet in person. The dating site is there to protect your personal information and you. If someone is insulted by you withholding your email address or phone number, simply ask them what advice they would give their sister or daughter in this situation. Most people understand the need for privacy and security. If they do not understand, then question if this is someone you wish to date anyway.

Some people like to talk on the phone before meeting, allowing them to get a better sense of the other person's personality, communication style, and compatibility. While I would agree with this, you have to decide if it is worth giving out your phone number. If you choose the phone over the computer, use a number that will not reveal your address. Cell phones are a little more secure, but for a fee on the internet, someone can still use a cell phone number to reveal an address. Cell phones do have the capability to block a particular phone number if ever needed. When you block a phone number, the person can still leave a voicemail, but to see this, you need to view your blocked messages. The blocked caller cannot text you, FaceTime you, or call you directly. Landlines are a "Do Not Use," but I am not sure if anyone still has a landline phone. Unwanted phone calls are the number one complaint from women using online dating sites, so just be a little cautious before handing out your phone number.

On average, after a few weeks of emailing/talking, you should have a basic interest in meeting this person. If you do not, move on to the next profile. If you do, it is time to set up a meet and greet, thereby avoiding a pen-pal. If someone continually avoids a face-to-face meeting, they are hiding behind the computer. In this event, they are most likely not who they portrayed themselves to be, are not interested in a relationship, or are married.

It is estimated that 30% of online users are married. If you are separated and not fully divorced, you are still married. People may be seeing what is "out there" before deciding to proceed with a separation or divorce. Some people will not get out of their current situation until they have a new person to be with. I am not judging these people, just asking for transparency.

I have found that people pending a divorce think they are ready for another serious relationship immediately, but feel differently once their divorce is final. This sentiment has been echoed by others who dated someone during a separation. Once the divorce was final, the newly divorced person felt they needed time to regroup and find themselves again. The term "rebound relationship" has been coined for the first relationship after a major life-altering event, like a divorce or the death of a spouse.

People in a rebound relationship are unsure of what they want and are still heavily emotionally engaged in the past relationship. Undoubtedly, there are always exceptions to the rule. It is just something to keep in mind if you choose to venture into one of these relationships.

When you decide to meet someone, pick a safe public place. I prefer daylight hours, which can be difficult during the winter months. Under these circumstances, if your daylight hours are limited, consider saving a first meet until your day off. I have known women who bring someone along with them on their first dates. If you have a friend along, please arrive early and have him/her sit a safe distance from you. I would not admit to bringing someone with me, but instead indicate a chance meeting if necessary. Another option is to meet where a friend or acquaintance is working. That way, you have an ally should the occasion arise.

Letting a friend know your plans and checking in with them at a designated time is the most popular safety check. If your outing extends past this designated time, tell your date you have to check in or excuse yourself to the ladies' room. Check-ins can be a simple text, using a thumbs up, or a thumbs down emoji. It will only take a second to let your friend know you are still out, or that your outing has ended and you are safe. You can also use your check-in for an SOS phone call if you are seeking to end your outing early. An SOS early removal from a date should only be used in extreme circumstances. Full disclosure, your date will believe he is being ditched, so have a credible excuse prepared. However you use your check-in time, you will still want to check in again when you are back home safe and sound.

If you are driving to your meeting, park in a space that is not isolated from others. Some establishments have parking behind the building, which can be very isolating and set yourself up for a potentially dangerous situation. Try to park in front of the building or by the front door. If it is dark or will be dark when you leave, be sure to park under a light or in a well-lit area. Give some thought to where you will park before choosing a place to meet.

A first date should be one to two hours. Keep it simple. This is an introduction or as I call it, a meet and greet. Some ideas are lunch, a walk in the park, a game of mini-golf, happy hour for a drink, or a pet play date. I do not recommend dinner or anything expensive, which may lead to feelings of obligation or other expectations.

If you ever feel uneasy on a date, do not dismiss this as just your nerves. Trust your internal alarm. Do not leave the venue by yourself. Instead, ask the hostess or manager to escort you to your car. I did this once. My date gave me a bad case of the creepy crawlers. I was embarrassed walking up to the manager at first, but he immediately put me at ease. I explained I was on a blind date and felt uneasy. Simple as that, I was escorted out to my car. A little embarrassment was quickly replaced with relief. You can cover quickly by telling your date you know the manager and are going to take a moment to chat on the way out to the car. If there is not anyone at the venue to assist you, wait for another group of people to leave and time your departure with them. That way you are not walking out by yourself. The goal, however you are able to achieve it, is to safely get to your car and home.

When driving home after meeting someone for the first time, check your rearview mirror to make sure you are not being followed. If you are ever in doubt, drive to your local police department. If someone is following you, they should abandon any idea of foul play once they see your new destination. Do not drive home until you are comfortable that you are safe. To repeat: **always trust your inner voice** when you feel something is amiss.

Enter your local police department's phone number as a contact in your cell phone so that you can dial them directly and eliminate the extra step of an emergency dispatcher. Of course, if you are out of your local area, dial 911. I was surprised at how long a 911 phone call can take. When you dial 911, you are connected to an emergency dispatcher. These dispatchers can cover a lot of territory, depending on the population in a given area. First, they need to know your location and the nature of your emergency, as it is their job to prioritize the phone call or emergency. Once the type of an emergency is established, the dispatcher will connect you with the local fire, police, and/or emergency medical service. The number of phone calls they are handling will determine your place in line. Think of it as going to the hospital emergency room, where a gunshot victim has priority over a sprained ankle. I called 911 to report a suspected drunk driver weaving all over the road one evening. Unfortunately, by the time I spoke with the local police, the driver was no longer in my view. I am not sure if the police ever did find this person. Hopefully, that person made it home safely and did not hurt anyone. After that incident, I entered the local police number in my cell phone and keep it there to this day.

Last but not least, before you go to an isolated area with this person, do one last security check for safety. By isolated areas, I am referring to meeting at your home, visiting his home, getting in a car with only him, or any situation where things can turn wrong very quickly. Before any of these situations might occur, you should know his full name, address, and birth date. Once you have this information, you can conduct a full internet search looking for any major red flags. You will be surprised at what information is available on the internet, with just this limited information. If nothing else, you will confirm this person is who he says he is. There are also sites for a nominal fee that will give you a full background check. Using one of these sites depends on how much you wish to know upfront.

I do not mean to be an alarmist, and sincerely hope this chapter has not scared you away from online dating. Most people are seriously seeking their match when dating, and the chances of anything bad happening are very slim. Most of the crimes committed online are cyber-related, where someone is trying to obtain your identity for their financial gain. However, if you watch the news, you will occasionally hear a story where someone met a very bad person online, and things ended poorly. Do not let that one statistic happen to you. Be careful and be vigilant. Take these safety tips to heart. Better safe than sorry.

Step 4
Grocery List

Yes, we all deserve the six-foot-tall handsome CEO of a major corporation who can buy us diamonds and a multi-million-dollar house or two! The reality is, there are not enough of these men for everyone, so in this case, you may have to re-examine your expectations.

There is no such thing as a real live breathing human Mr. Perfect. This is just a simple fact of life. There is a Mr. Perfect doll in the novelty stores, but I am hoping your aspirations are a little higher than that. With this in mind, it is time to make a list of your true deal-breakers and to examine areas where you can make some concessions. Are these deal-breakers based on tangible constraints or moral and ethical constraints?

Too many times, you may miss out on a great person because of a preconceived notion. Take a moment to think about where your deal-breakers are coming from. Are these deeply rooted in how you were raised, or are these assumptions or ideas recently formed? Recently formed ideas are much easier to re-examine versus lifelong concepts.

Similarly, tangible constraints are easier to make concessions with than moral or ethical constraints.

A major physical constraint seems to be height. Online dating has resulted in females focusing obsessively on a male's height requirement, causing men to "fib" about their true height. Tik-Tok has coined a phrase the "Short King," celebrating shorter men and challenging the height bias. With the short king movement, perhaps popular opinion will be in shorter men's favor very soon.

The average height for a man in the United States is 5'9", and globally it is 5'8". With these facts, asking for your match to be 6' tall reduces your possible matches to a very small percentage. If you are a woman who wishes her man to be taller than herself, consider wearing flat-heeled shoes or a smaller heel. This is a very simple solution you can implement to alleviate the height issue, and your feet will thank you! Many women say they raise their height requirement for a man because men exaggerate and are always 2 inches shorter than they say. This logic has now created a vicious cycle where men feel they need to say they are taller. In addition, now you are punishing the man who was honest and listed his height accurately. I challenge you to broaden your search a couple of inches downward on the height requirement. Let's give the honest man a chance, and do not assume he is fibbing about his height. This slight difference can increase your pool of men exponentially. Besides, everything lines up when you are lying down!

A disputable barrier for some women is a person's education level. A college degree does not necessarily measure your intelligence. Bill Gates, Mark Zuckerberg, Richard Branson, and Simon Cowell are just a few famous and highly successful people without a college degree. Some college graduates lack motivation and do not succeed in the working world. For instance, a college degree in basket weaving may not support a lavish lifestyle, yet he can still answer honestly to having a degree. For some, the cost of college may be or become a factor. You may meet a person without a current college degree but working towards one. Furthermore, he might be using tuition reimbursement from his current job to defer the astronomical cost of college. A person may not currently have a college degree but is fiscally intelligent which could result in being a good provider. On the flip side, you may meet a college graduate with mounds of debt, something to consider, especially if this relationship blossoms; you might be assisting in paying back his debt someday. Another cogent fact is that a portion of people have a career in something unrelated to their actual degree and never used the degree they earned. Second career choices have been on the increase since 2020, with middle-aged people in the income bracket of $50,000 to $75,000 leading this group. Many highly stressful careers are being exchanged for a career that brings pleasure. For these individuals, it has become more important to enjoy what they are doing for a living than to earn a large salary. A prime example of this is working on Wall Street, where analysts and associates often put in eighty to one-hundred hours every week. Mark Twain said, "Find a job you enjoy doing, and you will never have to work a day in your life." Be open-minded concerning an education level. A college degree does not equal happiness or necessarily a high-paying job. This sentiment is being reflected in the younger generations' feelings regarding college altogether. Currently, only 1 in 4 of this population feels a college degree will yield a high-paying position. It will be intriguing to see if the pendulum will swing toward more people not going to college and electing for a trade instead.

Trades are extremely undervalued until you need their services. I am referring to electricians, plumbers, carpenters, masons, etc. Once you own a home, these skills are invaluable. My first husband

and his father were very handy, building an addition to our home and doing all of our home repairs. I cannot even fathom the amount of money they saved by not contracting out these jobs. When they were no longer around, the sticker shock of having to hire someone for minor home projects was mind-boggling. Their skill level was something I took for granted, which resulted in my determination to learn how to do my simple home repairs. YouTube tutorials became my best friend, followed closely by Home Depot classes and, of course, asking a lot of questions from every accessible male I could find. I did give my neighbors a good laugh when I was on my roof cleaning the gutters in a skirt or while my neighbor and I put flower boxes on my second-floor windows. The latter was an episode right out of "I Love Lucy!" A good craftsman will always be in demand regardless of the economy. On the whole, they have job security and are usually their own boss. Furthermore, physical work can keep your man in shape. No gym membership is needed.

There is significant research that shows a correlation between IQ and compatibility. This research shows that couples with IQ scores within 30 points of each other are more likely to have shared interests and meaningful conversations. The problem here is most people do not know their IQ score, unless they belong to Mensa. Mensa requires an IQ of 132 or greater and is a club within itself. So unless you belong to Mensa or went to an Ivy League school, I cannot see this as a great opening conversation question. Asking for your IQ score is not the kind of question that will resonate well with most people. Interestingly, when men and women were asked to estimate their partner's IQ, both sexes overestimated. Women overestimated their partner's score by 38 points, and men overestimated their partner's score by 36 points. My take away here is to explore the person: you are not dating a piece of paper or a number.

"Geographically Undesirable" is a term even I am guilty of using, going back to location being a major stumbling block. We all have busy lives and find our days fill up quickly between working full time, raising children, going back to school, trying to get to the gym, or attending to whatever obligations and responsibilities you have. There are not enough hours in the day. On top of that, we become creatures of habit and tend to stay within a certain radius of our homes. One-third of people will not date outside of their neighborhood or city, while the other two-thirds of people enter a 30-mile radius or less when stating the distance they are willing to travel for their match. In most cases, this does not cover very much territory and may need to be revisited.

Look at what towns have a larger single population in your area. Towns that host singles tend to have more apartments, condos, and townhouses than large single-family homes. I do know a few women who relocated from predominantly couples or a double-income town to a town that held more single people, which resulted in finding a match. Generally speaking, there are more single women on the East Coast and more single men on the West Coast. Age also plays an important role in the percentage of single men. Under the age of 34, you will find a higher percentage of single men to women; however, this pattern starts to change after the age of 35, and every year, the number of single men to women lessens throughout the older years.

In 2024, the 5 best cities to find single men, according to Paired Life, are as follows:

1. Seattle, Washington: 134 single men per 100 single women. The highest concentration of single people is in the 30 – 40-year-old group.

2. San Francisco, California: 133 single men per 100 single women. The highest concentration of single people is in those over 40 years old.

3. San Jose, California: 132 single men per 100

single women. The highest concentration of single people is in the 20 – 40-year-old group.

4. Denver, Colorado: 125 single men per 100 single women. The highest concentration of single people is in the 30 – 50-year-old group.

5. Austin, Texas: 120 single men per 100 single women. The highest concentration of single people is in those under 50 years old.

The 2018 census revealed there were only 10 states that had more men than women. Alaska, Wyoming, and North Dakota are the three states with over 51%. Alaska has the highest percentage of men at 52.4%. This does not mean you need to pack up your belongings and move to one of the above locations, especially since these percentage deviations are not that large. However, you do need to factor in your surroundings. Women also must accept the fact that there are more women than men in the USA. As a woman ages, this percentage increases exponentially. One way to increase your pool of available men is to increase your searchable distance.

My Mr. "Not-So" Perfect lived 65 miles (75-minutes) away from me when we first met. I kept telling him he lived too far away. Initially, he made the trips down to see me since he was retired while I was still working full time. As I got to know him, the distance did not seem as important as I originally thought. Eventually, we started taking turns commuting on the weekends. The 75-minute drive was time to unwind after a busy work week, in fact I even started to look forward to the drive as my transition to the weekend. Happily, I am glad he was persistent! Needless to say, it was not the last time he proved me wrong.

Another tangible constraint that attracts a lot of attention is age. Ladies are notorious for seeking someone their age or older, within a three to five-year range. The age stigma is a thing of the past, so please re-think this and expand your age range to include younger men. Besides, when you get older, you can retire early, and your younger man will still have healthcare benefits through his job. Something to think about with the rising cost of healthcare. Men have no problem dating a younger woman; so why should women have a problem dating a younger man? I am not referring to winter/summer relationships, although there are cougar sites, if that is what you are seeking. Think of your ideal age range, and then add a few years on *both* sides of this range.

When does age enter into the equation when

finding a mate? One instance is when someone is considering marriage. Age matters more when looking at a long-term commitment versus if someone is considering a one-night stand. Another instance is the current stage of your life and your feelings towards children. Are you seeking to have children, or are you an empty nester wishing to keep it that way? When looking at a large age discrepancy, consider the future, since aging is a part of life.

For example, a 40-year-old man dating a 20-year-old woman has no trouble staying active and virulent. Unfortunately, this may be a different story when the same man is 70-years-old, and his wife is 50. (Of course, there is Mick Jagger, who fathered a child at the age of 73 with his girlfriend, then age 29. They just recently celebrated their child's sixth birthday.) That being said, I know several people who are very happy with a larger age difference. One friend explained she would rather be with her partner for whatever time they had together than be without him at all. They have a 23-year age difference and have been together for many years. Perhaps consider a person's energy or activity level, if age is not a deal breaker for you.

The great thing about dating is that it gives you a chance to decide if you are compatible with someone regardless of their age. Take this time to try something new. Generally speaking, do not let someone's age be the reason you deny yourself a chance at happiness.

Now, let's make your grocery list of the important things you would like in your match. When you make a grocery list, you list things that please you, taste good, give you comfort, and make you smile. Try making this type of list, focusing on character traits and qualities. Compatibility depends on a wide range of significant factors, including emotional intelligence, empathy, communication skills, and the ability to connect with others. Hone in on a few of these that are most important to you.

A few thoughts for a "new" grocery list might be:

➢ Makes you laugh.

This was always #1 on my list. Life can be hard, and someone who can make you laugh when times are tough is priceless.

➢ Is kind to others.

There is a saying that how a man treats his mother is how he will treat his wife or significant other.

➢ Supports your endeavors, wishes, or dreams.

You would like someone to make you a better

person, expose you to new experiences, and partake in experiences you can offer him. This way, you both grow.

➢ Enjoys similar interests.

Couples that play together, stay together. You do not need to do everything together. Having your interests and maintaining your friends is vital, but you do need to enjoy a few activities together.

➢ Effectively communicates.

So many early relationships fail due to communication styles or expectations. Discuss how often you need to talk, text, or be in touch when you start dating. One person may feel that daily communication is needed, whereas the other person feels weekly is sufficient. There is nothing wrong with asking "When would you like to talk again?" This will avoid the stress of whether he will call or not. You may still be disappointed if you don't receive the awaited phone call, but now you have a timeline and are not left in limbo.

Communication is one area you will work on throughout your entire relationship, so you might as well start discussing it from the beginning.

Next, it is time to review your new list, which should have the positive characteristics you are seeking. These positive attributes should be included in the body of your profile since you have identified these as important to your relationship.

Finally, have you expanded your mind by removing some preconceived notions? Does this new list allow you to explore new people? If whatever you have been doing has not yielded your match so far, perhaps it is time to remove some barriers and explore some new options. You do not have to remove all of these barriers at once.

Try starting with the barrier that is least frightening to you and move it just a little. If that is the age, try two years younger and older than you previously thought. If that is height, try one inch shorter. Remember, do not punish the honest person. Open your education restrictions. Increase your distance from 30 miles to 45 or 60 miles. Let's see if Mr. "Not-So" Perfect shows himself now!

Step 5
Swipe Right, Swipe Left

Prior to swiping (which is explained later), you will set your preferences for which profiles you would like to see. This is where you will enter whether you are seeking a female or male, the age and height range, distance from a designated zip code, and on some dating sites if you have a specific education level requirement. This will then show you the profiles of the people you have specified. The narrower the preferences, the lower the number of profiles you will see (which we discussed in detail in the previous step). Some people start with very strict preferences and expand as needed. As a general rule, this group of people with strict preferences leans towards searching for their match themselves. In contrast, some people cast a very wide net when selecting their preferences and see who responds to their profile, taking a more passive role in searching for their match. The choice is yours.

Once a profile is presented to you, you either swipe right or swipe left. Swiping is a fast way of stating your interest. Swipe right if you accept or extend the invitation to communicate further. Swipe left if you reject or decline the invitation to communicate further. You may swipe right, but unfortunately, if the other person swipes left, no further communication will be allowed. If both of you swipe right, then communication lines will be open through the dating site. This groundbreaking feature was developed by Tinder in 2012. Think of swiping as a quick hello. If the other person says hello, then you are invited to say something more.

Do not base your swiping direction solely on the photo. Take time to read the person's profile, for all of the reasons previously discussed in our grocery list, keeping in mind you would like a connection beyond the physical traits. I am the first to admit you do need a level of attraction to a person physically, but remember, a photo is very one- dimensional. If you do not want to put a bag over the person's head, read further!

Besides, attraction is visual but also involves all of your other senses, which you cannot experience through a photo. Try to break out of your "type." If you have always dated people with dark hair, try a blonde or redhead instead. We previously discussed in Step 2 how men are not the most insightful when it comes to placing their photos online, so if you are feeling kindhearted, explore those poor-quality photos.

Online dating can create a feeling of "Is there someone even better out there?" with so many people to choose from. Online dating can be compared to a kid in a candy store who can only choose one item, so before they choose, they sample everything until they have a stomachache. Perpetual daters have coined the expression "serial daters". Serial daters just like dating and will find any reason to dismiss a person because they want to see who's next. It is a case of the grass being greener on the other side. If this describes you, that is fine; just be honest with your feelings, and do not take advantage of people. You can state "casual dating only" or "just looking for a friendship" on your profile.

When you first create a profile, you may get inundated with potential matches requesting to communicate with you. This is because you are the new kid on the block or the shiny new penny, aside from being a fabulous catch. Some dating sites will flag you as "new" when you first enter, allowing men to dismiss people they have already reviewed. People also like to have to have the newest item. I still don't understand standing in line for the newest cell phone, but for some people, you may be the newest cell phone. On the contrary, if you are having difficulty making connections, remember people enter and exit the dating site every day, and you only need that one special person.

Seasons of the year will also play into your dating activity. Winter is the slowest season. When the weather is cold, people tend to hibernate. January is particularly slow while people recuperate from the holidays, both financially and physically, by getting back on their diet and exercise programs. February and Valentine's Day may bring a bit of activity, but some will not want the pressure of a new relationship colliding with this holiday centered around love. The majority of people will wait for March. The dating season always began for me with Saint Patrick's Day; since it's the first major event in the new year for people to come out and play. So don some green, and may the luck of the Irish be upon you!

Spring is the most active season for dating. People are coming out of their houses after the long winter months looking for excitement and romance; that's why spring is called the season of "rebirth." In the classic movie "Bambi," Owl says, "Nearly everyone gets twitterpated in the springtime." Flowers are blooming, and everything is new and budding, including romance. A lot of new profiles will be created during the springtime, resulting in an excellent time of year to jump into the dating world.

Summer is the time for steady dating. If you were fortunate enough to have met someone, continue your new romance through the summer months at a slow leisurely pace. If you are still searching, this is when a summer romance may pop up. Vacations or summer homes can add a new element of excitement. If you are going on a vacation or a weekend getaway alone, try searching online for someone at your destination. A local person may suggest the area activities or places to dine. Who knows, he may even join you for a glass of wine or offer to be your tour guide. While taking vacation photos, ask the available gentleman to take your picture for you. It will turn out better than a selfie and may initiate a conversation. A fan-favorite movie depicting a summer romantic partner that surprisingly shows up back in their hometown is "Grease." Many a summer romance may blossom into a long-term commitment, so don't rule one out.

Fall is harvesting time and another popular time for dating. Aside from the springtime months, October is the most popular dating month. Perhaps it is the last time to get outdoors to enjoy the weather and various activities like apple picking or hiking under the foliage. People are also preparing for the upcoming holidays and long winter nights ahead; where they would like to have a partner to snuggle with. The latter half of September and the month of October are safe distances from the holidays, leaving enough time to ascertain if you wish to enjoy the holidays with this person. Once Thanksgiving is in sight, it becomes more difficult, but not impossible, to start a new relationship.

Break away from being held hostage to these seasons. Think of your own seasonal feelings and activities. When are you the most open to meeting someone or feeling you would like a partner? Do you limit your search to certain months? Another way of thinking is that people are more committed to finding a match during the off- season peaks, so you might increase your swiping right during these off months.

I know on a cold winter day, it is harder for me to leave the house for a date. I imagine this is true for others, so if two people are willing to go out on a cold winter day, then they are committed to finding a relationship, or at the very least, committed to meeting each other. Of course, winter is the perfect season if you are a skier or enjoy winter hobbies, so break out your parka and enjoy a hot toddy after a day playing in the cold. Once again, I defied the norm by meeting both of my life partners in January.

People will and do connect all year long.

Limit the number of people you swipe right with, or you may end up trying to communicate with more people than you have time for. This is especially true if you are new to the site, or if it is spring and early fall. Women tend to feel overwhelmed by the number of responses, while men tend to feel insecure over the number of responses.

Several online dating sites will limit the number of times you can swipe right in a specific period. If you wish to exceed this number, you must pay a fee. If you are reaching the threshold of swiping right, I would have to conclude you are not taking enough time to read the profiles, or your search preferences need to be adjusted.

Who swipes first is an interesting concept. In 2014, a group of businesswomen created Bumble. Bumble's online dating app differentiated itself by only allowing women the ability to make the first move in heterosexual relationships. Women found this very appealing, because it removed unwanted contact from men, leaving them with a sense of empowerment. If your preference is to allow men an opportunity to make the first contact, do not worry as there are plenty of other sites. Different sites have various statistics on the percentage of females versus males that are swiping right or left. Does it matter who swiped first? Is this something you will even remember? You are only looking for that one person where both of you swiped right. If you see someone you think you might be interested in, what is wrong with saying hello? Think of swiping right as just saying hello. You are not committing to anything, but only offering a friendly gesture. If this person says hello back, wonderful! If they do not say hello back, it does not matter, since you do not know them anyway. So swipe right - be fearless!

Step 6
Kindergarten

In kindergarten, we learned the golden rule: "Treat others as we wish to be treated". It is a very simple life lesson.

When communicating online, some people forget they are dealing with a human being who has feelings and emotions. Cyberbullying, although noted in teenagers, will occasionally spill over onto an adult. Sadly, most of these adults do not feel their negative, aggressive comments even constitute bullying. I am always surprised at the number of people who use social media as a platform to preach or protest. This is not the proper time or place to get into political or social arguments. I understand fact-finding to see if your moral or ethical values align, but if not, then accept the fact that different people have different viewpoints. You are not looking to convert someone; you are looking for someone with similar viewpoints or someone who will have a rational adult conversation. If you cannot have a civil conversation online, simply acknowledge your differences, agree to disagree, and move on.

Upon meeting someone in person, you may feel

he is not a match for you, but that does not allow you to be rude. It is time to turn lemons into lemonade. Besides, you already set aside this hour of your time, got dressed, and primped for the encounter, so why not make the best of it? Sometimes, people are placed in your path for a different reason than you originally imagined. If you are a spiritual person, take a moment to see why you were meant to meet this person at this particular time. Is there something new this encounter taught you, or did meeting this person prompt you to not take for granted the next person you meet? Sometimes, we have to kiss a lot of frogs to appreciate the toad we fall for.

Another lesson we learned in kindergarten was to share. If this date is not for you, can you think of a single friend who might enjoy their company? I met a gentleman once who, unbeknownst to me, was a bit older. Yes, he fibbed on his profile, shocker! However, he was a good conversationalist with varied interests. I immediately thought of my friend, who was more age-appropriate. Subsequently, I introduced them, and they struck up a nice friendship. This gentleman hosted wine-tasting and bird-watching events, which I was then invited to attend. This broadened my social circle by introducing me to some new people, wine, and birds. Currently, we all maintain a friendship to this day.

Sometimes, an encounter can lead to both male and female friendships. In turn, these new friendships may lead to Mr. "Not-So" Perfect. Keep in mind Kevin Bacon's six degrees of separation theory, and try putting that to the test.

Profile misrepresentation or exaggeration is a common complaint. I believe you should be honest from the beginning about everything in your profile, excluding safety tips. Why would you want to start a new relationship on fibs? Also, when you meet someone in person, they will see you did not represent yourself correctly, prompting you to defend yourself or tell more fibs. While misrepresentation happens, I understand the frustration of the honest person and still have compassion for the person "stretching the truth".

I met a man whose picture was at least 15 years old, showed him to be 50 pounds lighter, and with a full head of hair, not a very bad toupee. While meeting this person, my close friends came into the same restaurant for lunch. Later they asked me why I didn't immediately turn around and walk out upon discovering this gross misrepresentation. My answer is two-fold:

First is compassion. If a person is so lonely they exaggerate to this extent just to have some human contact, then can I not offer some compassion? Will it hurt me to be kind, have a conversation, maybe learn something I did not know, and expand my mind? Remember, it is only for an hour or two, and I am already there.

Second, I did not like it when someone treated me rudely. Twice, I was mortified while on a first date. The first time, I sat at the table in the bar area of a chain restaurant and ordered a glass of wine while waiting for my date. This person (I am not calling him a gentleman) walked in, asked me my name, and then sat down. After sixty seconds, he looked at me and said, "No, you are not for me," got up and left. I pride myself on being honest on my profile, including my real age, height, and current pictures, so his behavior left me wondering how I could have been misleading. I had already told the server I was meeting someone. I believe she and other patrons witnessed this whole event, adding to my embarrassment. I asked for my check and left immediately, feeling like the whole world was watching me.

The second time, I met a person at our local pub, where I knew the bartenders and some of the patrons. I wore a cute dress and thought I looked nice. This person (again, not a gentleman) walked in, asked me my name, and then proceeded to tell me I was not the dress size I proclaimed to be. I remember asking him if he wanted to see the tag on my dress to prove I had told the truth. He informed me it did not matter because he wanted someone smaller than me and left. His words zeroed in on one of my major insecurities, as weight issues have plagued me since I was a child. On a side note, I was a size 6, but that did not matter because, in my mind, this person told me I was fat and transported me back to my childhood. Thank goodness I found a neighbor, and we commiserated on how hurtful some people can be.

I could give you several more stories where I did not have great experiences, but I believe you grasp my message. Pat yourself on the back that you were kind and made someone's day. Kindness is contagious. Spread it a little and watch it grow. Kindness doesn't cost a thing and is gravely needed in the world.

Do not become argumentative while on a date. Becoming upset or angry will not serve you well. A first meeting with someone is not the time to tell this person he lied, wasted your time, or to voice any harsh words. This is a stranger who may anger easily and respond unfavorably. You do not want to accidentally push the wrong buttons, bringing out aggression. Avoid confrontation at all costs. Once more, safety should be your main concern. You can rant and rave to a girlfriend later.

At the same time, if you do not have any interest in this person and he is interested in you, be honest and tell him. A simple statement saying you do not feel this is a good match and thanking him for his time is sufficient. You do not need to go into detail explaining why. If he persists or asks for a reason, a safe response is you do not feel the chemistry or a romantic interest. Take the onus for this encounter not working: do not make it personal. There is enough cruelty in the world. If you do not feel comfortable turning down someone in person, then send him a message when you get home using the dating site. In most situations, it is easier and safer to send an email the next day, again being kind. I always wished both of us luck in our continued search, indicating I am also sad this encounter did not work out.

You may share constructive and positive feedback if you honestly feel your feedback will help this person find his match. It could be that you found something appealing about this person, encouraging them to add that in their profile verbiage. An example of this might be something like, "I did not realize you were an avid cyclist. I am sure other cyclists would like to know this about you and share your passion." If this person had a poor or outdated photo, you may wish to say something like, "Your picture does not do you justice. You are so much more handsome in person. Have you given any thought to an updated photo?" (If you like this person, you may want to keep that example to yourself. After all, you did not let a bad photo deter you from meeting him.)

Above all else, ghosting is rude! Ghosting is when someone disappears without any contact at all. Here one second, gone the next, leaving you wondering where they went. We all know what it is like waiting for that phone call, text, or email. The anticipation can be nerve-wracking, especially if you like this person. A simple email is another act of kindness and just plain good manners.

Online dating may bring some negative comments or criticism. You will need to have resilience or a thick skin, and try not to take things personally. If someone is mean, this is not a person you wish to associate with anyway. Be thankful you saw this trait and saved any further investment of your time and energy. You are very brave putting yourself out in the dating world, and rejection even from someone you had absolutely no interest in may still be a little hard on the ego. It is not a reflection on you; it just was not your match. Do your best to turn your negative experiences into positive learning experiences. This is not to say everyone will have negative experiences. You might be very fortunate and have only positive experiences or even better, meet your match on the very first date.

Step 7
Three Strikes Before You're Out

A baseball player gets three strikes before he is out. Try using this analogy for your dates. First dates can be difficult. In many cases, a person can be nervous, have had a bad hair day, or may just take time to warm up to someone.

The only thing a first date should reveal is if you enjoyed each other's company enough to have a second date. Would you care to spend another hour or two with this person? That's all. It is not, "Where will this lead? Do I see myself with this person for the rest of my life?" Unquestionably, those assumptions are way too premature.

Now, if you want to run away from this first date screaming, then it is a nice "thank you, but no thank you" to further dates. If you say to yourself he was nice, but I did not feel instant chemistry, then I say give him three strikes, which means another date.

The chemistry people think of upon initially meeting someone is really infatuation, not love. Infatuation tends to dissipate over time owing to the fact that it is usually based on superficial attributes. A 2001 movie, "Shallow Hal", starring Jack Black, features a jerk who only dates physically perfect women. After a run-in with a self-help guru, Hal is hypnotized to see beauty in the least physically appealing woman. This movie illustrates the concept that beauty is only skin deep and love can grow. Your "aha" moment can still come down the road after you get to really know someone. In fact, when you may least expect it!

First dates should be short and sweet. It is an introduction, leaving the person wanting to know more about you. There is an art to having a conversation. By definition, a conversation is the spoken exchange of thoughts, ideas, observations, opinions, or feelings between people. Conversations should have a give-and-take and not be dominated by one person. Take turns talking, listening more than you talk. The quote, "We have two ears and one mouth, so we can listen twice as much as we talk," is a good philosophy to follow. Let this person know you are engaged in what they have to say by practicing active-attentive listening. People in general like to talk about themselves. Allow them to share what they wish, as opposed to asking a string of questions, resulting in an interrogation. There is a popular 21-question game online that gives you some lively ice-breaking questions to get a conversation rolling. Having one or two of these ready for an awkward pause is not a terrible idea. Generally speaking, discuss your common interests, share a funny story, or ask them what is on their list of things they would like to do that they have not yet done. Just keep the conversation light and fun.

Elements a person looks for in a first date include your smile, self-confidence, punctuality, manners, body language, and authenticity. Demonstrate your self-confidence by making eye contact and smiling. As previously discussed under your photography tips, these qualities are also essential when connecting in person. Body language will let another person know immediately if you are interested. Lean into the conversation, and give a gentle touch on his arm. It's okay to flirt a little. Lastly and most importantly, be real, be you, and let your sunny side shine. This is a date, not an interview.

Punctuality shows respect while demonstrating good manners, especially on a first encounter. If for some reason you are going to be late, send a message apologizing and let him know your new estimated time of arrival. Then once you arrive, apologize again for your tardiness. This should be done if you are more than 5 minutes past your agreed-upon time. A good habit one of my friends implemented was arriving 15 to 30 minutes early not only to ensure her punctuality but also to scope out the area. Once, while waiting for her scheduled date, she met another single gentleman who asked her out. Talk about maximizing her time! She achieved an exacta, two dates for the outfit of one. I love that story: it just emphasizes the importance of being open to your surroundings. Life may surprise you!

While on a first date, people often worry about how to say goodbye. Remove this pressure by acknowledging that most first dates do not end in a kiss. If you really like someone, a kiss on the cheek is sufficient and sends this message without being overly sexual. If someone is physically all over you, question their motive by asking yourself if they are just looking for a one-night stand. If they invite you home, or to their hot tub on the first date, chances are they are not interested in your mind.

Men are not mind-readers, and most are not good at picking up subtle clues, which calls attention to the need for clear communication. Send a follow-up email telling him you enjoyed the meeting. Be confident and extend this courtesy. Forget the silly three-day rule. This old-fashioned etiquette required the woman to wait for the man to contact her. The man was expected to wait three days. Sooner was considered overzealous and later was considered an afterthought. The modern version of this rule has expanded to include a text or phone call the next day, and a second date a week later or whenever your busy calendars align. I would not recommend the woman always taking the lead in initial post-date contact, just after the first date. Men do like to be the pursuers, but sometimes, they need a little extra encouragement initially.

When I was in my early 20's, I had a function to attend where everyone was going to be attending as a couple. At this time, I was off again with my current boyfriend, so one day, I gathered up my courage and asked this cute guy if he would like to attend this event with me. I had never been so nervous in my life. It was akin to speaking in front of a large audience or stage fright. This cute guy was flattered and gently turned me down, but I remember wondering if this is what a man goes through when asking out someone he is interested in dating. Empathy: I am now acutely aware of the courage it takes to ask out another individual. If you would like to see your date again, make the invitation for a second date as painless as possible. During your conversation, leave a few openings or ideas for a second date. He will appreciate the gesture and hopefully pick up on your clues.

The second date will reveal a little more about both of you. Try to choose a different type of event or surroundings. For example, if you met for happy hour or lunch, try an activity this time. It is always helpful to have different types of interactions and see people in a different light. Humans are multifaceted, and choosing different settings will bring out a different layer of someone's personality. A second date may be a little longer in duration, but it is still not a marathon or all-day adventure. Think of something you would like to do that you might have postponed since you did not have someone to join you. Additionally, consider your commonalities since you want the second date to be enjoyable for both of you.

The only thing a second date should reveal is if you would like a third date. Do you like him enough to explore another outing with him? Again, you are not walking down the aisle; you are not promising him your kidney or any major commitment! A good question to ask yourself is, "Would you prefer going out with this person or staying home by yourself?" Sometimes, the answer is staying home by yourself. If staying home alone is not appealing, then give him a third date.

The focus of a third date should still be fun and an

opportunity to explore each other a bit further. Perhaps on this date, you choose something he enjoys that you are trying for the first time. Part of dating is new experiences. By trying something new you are not only showing an interest in something he likes, you are also showing flexibility and a willingness to grow. At this juncture, your conversations should have revealed some thoughts on various topics, indicating if your moral or ethical beliefs align. If you have not brought up any of your deal breakers, now is a good time to touch upon something you feel strongly about. Once again, you are not looking for an argument; you are just ascertaining his feelings on certain topics. Can you discuss politics without getting into a major disagreement? Religion? Any other hot social topic of today? Whatever the topic, can you both accept each other's responses? Can you laugh together at what the psychic says? You are still not ordering monogrammed towels. You are only determining if there were any deal-breakers or hidden prison tattoos.

By the end of your third date, this person should pique your interest to the level of "We are getting along" or "I find him intriguing." If after the third date, you are indifferent, it may be time to move on. Do not continue dating simply for something to do.

If you feel that way, then you have delegated him into the "friend" zone. It is always nice to have another friend, as long as you both feel the same way. Perhaps he's better suited for another single friend. You successfully experienced three dates and hopefully determined he is not a serial killer. Remember, we did learn to share in kindergarten!

If this person makes it past three dates without striking out, you have a real contender. Take your time and see if this person will move out of the awkward dating stage and into the attracted dating stage. We will discuss the dating stages in Step 10. Right now, get to know this person a little more on each additional date, in different surroundings, and, when the time is right, around your friends. Save the family introductions for last, when you are 100 % sure this person is a keeper. You do not wish to scare him away. We all know our families can be scary.

Step 8
Sabotage

Women can be their own worst enemy. We can self-sabotage at any moment, usually as a result of fear, including, but not limited to, fear of being rejected, fear of being hurt again, fear of commitment, or fear of intimacy.

If you are having a bad series of dates, perhaps it is not the fault of the people you are dating. In this situation, try taking a moment to re-examine your dates for how you participated in these interactions. Could you have a role in why these dates might not have gone well? Sometimes, this introspective look may take a bit of soul searching; however, until you face your fears, it is difficult to move forward. An interesting question to ask is, "Would you like yourself if you met yourself?" You need to like who you are before asking another person to like you. Of course, there are a lot of unsuitable matches out there. You may just be unlucky; even so, it does not hurt to take a look at ourselves periodically for areas of improvement.

According to Psychologists Today, there are several areas in which a woman can disrupt their dating experiences. Let's see if any of these are areas you might need to address for better dating results or to enhance your current dating relationship.

Are you expecting the man to take the lead all of the time? A relationship is give and take, including some reassurance and participation from the woman. In comparison, a job or project can be overwhelming if you feel you are carrying the workload of another person. Did you ever encounter a work colleague who didn't contribute his share? How did that make you feel? This is also true with dating. Very few men are looking for June Cleaver from "Leave it to Beaver." Although, they may not object to a red evening dress, slippers and pipe at hand, and dinner sizzling on the table. Perhaps you can save that for a special event or (more likely in my case), April Fool's Day. In the interim, you can always ask him if he would like you to plan a date since he has planned the last few. If you are uncomfortable planning a date, at least reassure him you appreciate his efforts in planning these outings for you. Compliment his creativity, his choice of restaurants, or the type of activity he planned for both of you. Surprise him by giving him something thoughtful as a thank you. It does not have to be anything expensive, just a token of your appreciation or a gesture, like helping him wash his car. A wise man once said, "After unlocking your date's car door and seeing she is seated, observe if she reaches over and unlocks your door for you while you are walking around the car. If the woman unlocks your car door, then she is a keeper." Be the woman who reaches over and unlocks the door. There are many different ways to participate and be an active contributor in a relationship.

Are you sharing all of your problems and looking for sympathy? If so, you will receive better guidance from a licensed therapist. Please do not discuss your ex, and do not under any circumstances say anything negative about your ex. Ex-boyfriend or ex-husband discussions always look like you have not moved on and still harbor bitterness. If you are asked, answer politely with a brief comment and change the subject. Another difficult hurdle to overcome is to not compare current dates to someone from the past. The person you are comparing them to is in the past and does not exist any longer. If they did exist, they would still be with you. Exes are a minefield best to be avoided at all costs. Discussing the other areas in your life where you are unhappy is also a minefield. If it is a bad work situation or a bad relationship with a friend or child, feel free to ask for input or advice, but do not dwell on negative situations. No one wants to be with an Eeyore. You may recall Eeyore from "Winnie the Pooh," is always saying woe is me.

Eeyore is gloomy, negative, and depressing, versus Tigger, who is always bouncing, optimistic, hopeful, and imaginative. Wouldn't you really rather be a Tigger?

Are you mirroring your date? I mean defaulting to your date's preferences almost to the point of mimicking him. A relationship is between two different people. If he wanted to date himself, he could have stayed home and talked to himself in the mirror. Not surprisingly, there is a term – narcissist - for someone who only wants a "yes" person. Initially, this might be the easy way to avoid conflict by agreeing to everything your partner says and does; however, it will not be sustainable for the long haul. People like to be needed, appreciated, and able to contribute their thoughts and ideas, which can only be achieved if you share your own thoughts and have an opinion. Ask your date what he thinks on a particular topic. Then, express your thoughts. You do not always have to agree with or believe in the other person's contribution, but you do need to validate his right to have one and to voice it. This is the basis for a good conversation. This is how we learn another perspective on various topics. As a result, opinions may change or broaden – his, or even yours. Eventually, every relationship has an argument or disagreement. If you cannot share your thoughts or feelings, you will internalize them, building resentment. Over time, this will lead toward a toxic relationship. Sharing your opinions is growth and vital to a successful relationship.

Are you showing your insecurities by constantly fishing for a compliment? Men like self-confidence. In fact, this is listed as their number one trait when seeking a partner. We all like compliments, but let them be given naturally. Consider your reaction if a man was consistently asking if he looked good in his shirt every time you saw him. Seeking a preference for one outfit over another is one thing, but always seeking approval is exhausting. I dated a bodybuilder in my youth. I remember thinking I was very lucky to have such a handsome specimen, until I realized there was not a mirror or reflection that he could walk past without checking himself out. I was not the right person to inflate his ego since I am much more relaxed about appearances. Trust that a man will not go out with someone he does not find attractive. Undoubtedly if this person is dating you, then, yes, he finds you attractive. Men like to receive compliments as much as women, so be sure to occasionally compliment him. If you feel the need for a compliment, offer one instead and see if it is reciprocated. Above all, avoid the dreaded question, "Does this make me look fat?" Every man in the world will tell you that question has no right answer.

Are you overindulging? By overindulging, I mean alcohol. Be mindful of your alcohol intake. As a rule, a drink or glass of wine should last one hour, while two drinks during your outing should be your maximum. This rule is valid in the business world and dating, especially the first stages of dating. I understand you might be nervous, and a glass of wine or a drink can calm you down. But alcohol is a double edged sword. Large amounts of alcohol may send the wrong message. Be conservative, especially while you are learning about a person. You can always let your wild side out later.

Are you relying on sex to build your relationship? Sex is an important part of any relationship but should not be the initial main focus. Once you have sex, it will quickly overshadow the relationship and become the main focus, which you may not intend. Remember, sex starts in the brain. It is a scientific fact that when sexually excited, a hormone called oxytocin is released. Oxytocin strengthens a bond between adults earning the nickname, "The love hormone." The more you learn about each other, the more powerful your sexual relationship will be. During sex, you are sharing a deep intimacy while surrendering and exposing your vulnerable side. For these reasons, I advocate holding off on sex for as long as you can. If you are looking for a monogamous relationship, please make sure he agrees to monogamy before you have sex. Discuss sex before you engage in sexual activity. This means before you're in the throes of passion. The classic song by Meatloaf called "Paradise by the Dashboard Light," rightfully explains that a man will agree to anything in the heat of the moment. If you cannot have this discussion, then you are proceeding without any knowledge of each other's level of commitment or sexual preferences. Is this an area of conservative behavior or an area of experimentation? Avoid embarrassment and misunderstandings by setting the ground rules first. Do not lead with sex and then expect everything else to fall into place. That is a recipe for heartbreak.

Are you expecting the man to pay for everything? Many women may feel splitting the bill is being treated with respect. If this is how you feel, tell the gentleman before ordering anything. Don't let it become a power struggle once the bill arrives. According to a recent survey of 300,000 American singles, 64% of men believed it's the man's responsibility to pay on the first date, while 46% of women agreed. This statistic did not disclose the age range of the people polled, so this may be a generational thought.

With the high cost of items, I feel we all need to be a little more cost-conscious while dating. One way to avoid paying while on a date is to find things that are free, like a walk on the beach, or in a park. Another way is to seek out very inexpensive activities. I know there are different thoughts on meeting for coffee. People have compared meeting for coffee with a drive-by encounter, but coffee can be combined with playing a board game to extend the encounter. I just met a couple that had bicycling dates through their local meet-up group. As a result, they are now living together and still bicycling away.

Age and status in life will play into the paying factor. A young man out of college living in an urban area will not date very much if he has to pay $20 for his date's glass of wine. A large portion of the younger generation feels that women should assist with the bill or reciprocate. If you offer to reciprocate, please follow through on your offer. Do not offer to pay for the next date, if you have absolutely no plans of having another date.

On the other extreme, I was very uncomfortable on a second date when I found out the restaurant my date chose was quite expensive. I did not believe this gentleman could afford this extravagant dinner, which was mistake number one and a total assumption on my part. I jumped to conclusions and felt pressured, so I derailed the entire relationship. I quickly brought up the dreaded question; "Are you looking for marriage?" To my surprise, he said he would not rule it out. I then countered this comment by stating I had no intention of getting married again. Talk about sabotaging! In retrospect, this was not a very good way of dealing with this situation. I should have taken the time to learn more about him instead of imagining all types of negative scenarios. I should have looked at this from a positive perspective, asking myself if this was his favorite restaurant. For all I knew, he was independently wealthy and trying to show me a lovely evening. I have no idea why he chose this restaurant because I did not take the time to find out. Alternatively, I could have researched the restaurant in advance and suggested a less expensive option. The blunt fact was that splitting this bill was outside my budget at that time. My bad behavior haunted me and led to some soul searching. I came to realize I did not give this man the respect he deserved. I probably let a good one get away.

Maybe you're like me, a bit old-fashioned and pleased when a man offers to pay. The key word is "offers". I feel that if a man offers to pay, it shows he likes you and is hoping for another date. Depending on the costs, you may offer to split the bill or offer to leave the tip. Perhaps you had an activity, and you offered to buy the post-activity ice creams. Something to contribute, anything to contribute. Men will feel that you appreciate them and are not out for their wallets.

Are you sabotaging your dates without even realizing it? Oh how our subconscious can play tricks on us. My friends used to tease me that once I cooked, my date ran for the hills never to be heard from again! To help me avoid that in the future, my dear neighbor, who is an excellent cook, cooked a dinner I passed off as my own. We did pull this off, even dirtying up my kitchen a little. The meal was excellent; however, the man stopped calling me immediately after this evening. Noticing a pattern, I resumed soul searching, realizing it wasn't the food, it was my attitude. Once this person came into my home, my personality changed. I did not want someone to invade my private space, so of course, the person did not feel welcomed. I learned to keep the dates outside of my home until I felt more secure. If I felt comfortable having them in my home, then I knew they had passed my first major obstacle toward a sustainable relationship.

Children can challenge or even sabotage a

relationship. If either of you have children, you need to ask, "Are your children ready for you to date again?" Take some time to discuss your re-entering the dating world with your children, regardless of their age. You may need to ask them open-ended questions to enlist a response. The question can simply be, "What does dating mean to you?" Above all else, listen to your children, and try to remove any of their concerns. Be open and honest with them.

The best advice I can offer is not to involve them in a relationship too early. If you are divorced or widowed, the children have already suffered a major loss. You do not want them to get attached, have the relationship not work out, and have them suffer another loss. This can be very emotional for any child, especially if your child accepted this person into their life, filling a major void. Try to keep the children out of your dating world until you are sure this is a committed monogamous relationship that you are both planning on taking long term. If your new partner also has children, having them meet each other and get along will be easier if all children know you are united and strong in your commitment.

Child care is expensive and might be difficult for you to budget into finances. If you have shared custody, date while your children are not with you. If you have full custody or the father is no longer involved, consider asking a family member in the area to help you. Possibly, you can barter with a friend. If you are bartering or scheduling "play dates" for your children, tell your friends your plans, making sure they are comfortable with you going on a date while they watch or entertain your children. You do not want your friends to feel you are taking advantage of them. Of course, bartering does mean you reciprocate. If your children attend activities like Boy Scouts or Girl Scouts, this may be your time to meet someone.

It can be tricky to carve out some dating time, but plenty of people figure it out. According to the 2023 US Census Bureau, 1,300 new step-families are formed every day. 40% of families in the US are blended, with at least one partner having a child from a previous relationship. A blended family is defined as any household that includes a step-parent, step-sibling, or half-sibling. The 70's television show "The Brady Bunch", which can still be found in syndication, depicts a blended family illustrating these life lessons. Remember "Marsha, Marsha, Marsha?" There are a lot of real-life Brady Bunches in this world, so something is working.

After your date, take some time to see if you are

intentionally or subconsciously sabotaging yourself. We all have walls that need to be taken down or obstacles we need to overcome. Call it baggage, call it whatever you wish, just figure it out and confront it. Why risk endangering a potentially promising relationship? Do not be too hard on yourself. Learn from your experiences and make adjustments for the future.

Step 9
Dating Fatigue

Dating takes a lot of energy and time. People have referred to it as a part-time or even a full-time job. Plainly speaking, if you feel this way, you are quickly heading toward dating fatigue. It does take time to read the profiles or find a club, achieve a level of comfort, and finally go on a date. All of this can be exhausting, and after some time, it may take a toll on you. First and foremost, you need to take care of your mental and physical health.

Dating fatigue might present as an attitude of indifference, a feeling of hopelessness, the thought of exhaustion if you have to go on one more date, or wanting to just give up on dating altogether. Some people will experience this after just a few dates, while others will not feel this for a few years. Nevertheless, most people will feel dating fatigue on and off over some time.

Engaging your friends with your dating adventures, both good and bad, is one way to ward off dating fatigue. We're not talking about the friends who say you are too picky or ask why you haven't met someone yet. Choose the friends you can laugh with and have some tomfoolery with to share your adventures. These are the friends who will help you keep your sense of humor and pick you up when you are feeling down. A couple of my friends looked forward to my dating tales, prodding me even when I was not in the mood to share. Thank goodness for girlfriends! We usually found something to laugh at, especially if the date did not go well. We would then come up with funny nicknames for these dates, not to be mean, but just to keep my sense of humor and give me the strength to keep trying. My friends kept reminding me, it only takes that one special person to change your world.

In any event, once you get to the point where you are no longer having a good time, you need to take a break. In sales, you are taught to smile when speaking on the phone so your positive mannerisms and positive energy are extended and hopefully reciprocated. This holds true with dating. If you are tired, it will show in your speech and personality. If you are not enjoying yourself, then neither will your date. Misery doesn't love company in the dating world, so give yourself a well-deserved break to re-group.

You can take a break in several different ways. Passive dating is leaving your profile visible, but only checking it for incoming mail once a week. You do not seek anyone out and only review a potential person if they contact you. Limiting your online time is the key: remember, you are on a break and should not be spending more than an hour or two every week during passive dating. Another way is to hide your profile and then reactivate it when you wish. If you hide your profile, no one will be able to see it, and no communication will be allowed. Similarly, some dating services allow you to freeze your membership. Just remember that freezing your membership will sever all communication. Both hiding and freezing your activity will remove your involvement, providing an absolute 100% break from online dating.

While you are taking this break, see if there are strategies you can implement when you are ready to get back in the game to avoid future dating fatigue. Some strategies include:

- Going to events for your enjoyment, not in the hope of meeting someone. This way the success of your evening is not based on meeting a man. Have a healthy ratio of fun times with family and friends versus dating with a purpose. This is important for your mental health. If dating feels like a job, then you are out of balance. Everyone aspires toward a well-deserved and balanced life.

- Evaluate your outlook on dating. Are you approaching dating like a scavenger hunt, searching for the golden ticket, or are you looking at dating as an opportunity for growth? Are you resistant to change, knowing that if you allow someone into your life, it will change? Dating should be a welcoming and exciting part of your life, resulting in new people and adventures. See if you can make peace with how you approach dating.

- How do you handle rejection or negativity? Resilience can be fragile. In lieu of internalizing someone's negativity, choose a positive affirmation. This affirmation should remind you that you are perfect in every way. This way you are placing the negativity back on the other person. One of my affirmations is: "You cannot shake hands with a clenched fist." It reminds me that I could extend myself all I wished, but the onus was on another. If that other was closed off to receiving, then there would be no shaking of hands. Find a saying or mantra that resonates with you. How about, "I am rubber, and you're glue: whatever you say bounces off of me and sticks to you." That one still makes me smile.

- Implement self-care with times that rest your mind. In other words, take mental time out. We all need to shut down our thoughts occasionally. It does not have to be a conscious effort like meditation or yoga, although I love both of these. It could be going for a walk, taking a bubble bath, crocheting, or reading a book, which are all active mind rests. Your mind can only hold one thought at a time. Proof of this is attempting to multitask. The term "multitasking" is, in fact, a misnomer. You are never truly focusing on two tasks at the same time. All you're doing is continuously switching between the two thoughts. Whether it is a positive or negative thought, you have the power to replace a thought at any time.

- Set a goal or make a game out of dating. Not a game at anyone's expense. I propose a game to motivate you and get you out of dating doldrums. For example, my goal is two dates a month, or I will swipe right twice a week, promising to be open to communicating with anyone who contacts me. This type of goal or game will keep you motivated and will also push you a little outside your comfort zone with your dating choices. If you meet your goal, reward yourself.

- Limit your travel on first dates. I know I said earlier to expand your distance and broaden your search, which is still advisable. Here, I am pointing out that if you are traveling far, your expectations will be much higher than traveling a reasonable distance. A simple solution is to share the distance by meeting halfway. You should not be the person doing 100% of the traveling. If the other person is not willing to meet you halfway, then he is not that interested in meeting you. Regardless of his words, actions speak louder. On the other hand, if he is willing to meet you halfway, see if there is an interesting new place both of you can explore. This way, if the date does not meet your expectations, you still have a day trip experiencing something new.

- Reschedule if you are too tired or do not feel well. Sometimes, life gets in the way of our best-laid plans. Several things can derail your week, such as unexpected obligations, a new deadline at work, or even a sudden illness.

Communicate the circumstances to your date, explaining that you want to be at your best when you meet. There is plenty of time for him to meet the tired, cranky side of you. While describing your circumstances and even admitting you are not in good spirits, have an alternative date ready. This way, you are not canceling but rather re-scheduling. Of course, give as much prior notice as humanly possible. No one understands last-minute cancellations, unless they involve a trip to the emergency room. Cancellations will lead the man to think you are no longer interested. Men are just as sensitive as women when it comes to perceived rejection.

I was suffering from very bad allergies and needed to cancel a second date with my now husband. I followed up with a phone call when I felt better and asked for another opportunity to pursue our planned rendezvous. It took me a bit to convince him that I was sick. He confessed to having previous people cancel a date at the last minute and not reschedule, so he was very skeptical. In hindsight, I should have had an alternative date ready when I canceled. What I did not confess was I had been looking forward to the activity he had planned. I was impressed he listened to me on our initial date and planned our second date based on a suggestion of mine. This thoughtful gesture was what led to our second date and, despite my error, many more years of being together.

- Explore other options besides online dating. Step 1. Discussed face-to-face initial meetings. Perhaps you shine in a different venue, allowing people to see your amazing personality. While on a break, try something different.

- Re-evaluate your online profile. Is there something off-putting in your profile? Maybe a different set of photos or different verbiage is needed. Take this time to mix it up a bit. Try a new approach or a new site. If you did not ask a man's advice before, ask for it now. Do not obsess over your profile; just see if there is something you can do a little better. Look at your parameters and see if you can open them a little wider. There is no shame in not finding your match within a certain period. The stars just have not aligned for you yet.

- Set a time to return to dating. Time has a way of slipping by very quickly. Like exercising, it is easy to stop and hard to start back up again. If you are taking a total break, make yourself a promise to re-enter the dating world in a specific time period and mark it on your calendar. You do not have to re-enter the online dating world. You just need to engage in the world and be open to meeting someone. If you are closed, your body language will display this without you even being aware. Schedule more win-win situations, events where you are excited about the outing, and if it works out with a man, then that is an extra added bonus.

When returning to dating, remind yourself to keep your eye on the prize. The prize is finding your match in spite of the distractions that may try to derail this goal. You are not alone if you do not like the whole dating process. Most people do not enjoy dating. However, it is a necessary evil if you want a relationship.

Step 10
The Dating Dance

Let us now presume your hard work has paid off and you have met someone you like. You have made it past the first three dates and decided to explore this individual further. This is when the dating dance begins.

There are several phases to dating or any relationship, which are listed below in chronological order. There is not a specific time for how long you stay in any phase. People can exit and re-enter a phase at any time, hence the dance.

First is the Awkward Phase: You have decided you both like each other. You have some common interests, or at least the interest to explore further. You are starting to feel comfortable with each other, but are unsure if this person is "the one." While getting to know each other, there will be some unexpected surprises or awkward moments. These moments are learning opportunities for both of you. Ask questions, listen to your partner, and get to know each other. Be your authentic self. Let your guard down. Continue your outside interests, but make regular plans. Discuss if you are going to focus on each other or continue to date other people. Please do not assume the other person is being loyal to you without verbal confirmation. Now is the time to address this before you are further invested.

<u>Second is the Attraction Phase or Honeymoon Phase:</u> This phase is very exciting. Here, everything is exciting and new. The flowers smell sweeter, and the sun is shining brighter. Cupid has shot you with his arrow. You are on your best behavior always wanting to put your best foot forward. You're starting to fall in love and want him to fall in love with you. Enjoy your time here, build your memories, and savor these moments now and later. Do not worry about when or if this phase will end. If it is meant to be, it will grow into something even stronger. Throughout your relationship, there will be times you revisit this phase. It may just be a fleeting moment when you experience an act of kindness and remember why you first fell in love. It could be a single event, like a romantic dinner at home or a special evening out. It might even be a weekend or week-long getaway, rekindling the romance while making time for a second, third, or fourth honeymoon. Revisit this phase as often as possible, remembering all the wonderful reasons you fell in love with this man.

Third is the Intimacy Phase: This phase is where you deepen your emotional and physical connections, which allow you to be vulnerable. Your conversations will start to become more meaningful by sharing not only your personal experiences, values, dreams, and aspirations, but also parts of yourself that are not ideal. In simple terms, this is when you share the good, the bad, and the ugly. Your defense mechanisms are being lowered. You are trusting this other person with your secrets, and they are trusting you with theirs. Linger for a while here since you are now becoming emotionally invested. There is no need to rush toward the next phase. As things naturally progress, you will be picking up his underwear off the floor soon enough! As with any meaningful conversation, take turns sharing intimacies. Invest the time to listen to your partner's stories and learn what has molded him into the person he is today. The more you learn, the better understanding you will have on how to support him.

During this time, you do not need to divulge everything about yourself all at once, and in the end, there may be some things you never share. If you have had some hardships in life, take care not to scare your partner away. You do not want to sabotage the relationship by being repeatedly negative or revealing too many horror stories at once. Discussing these negative experiences when a trigger situation occurs will offer your partner a better reference point and will help your partner understand why certain situations may affect you differently. Do not apologize for these experiences; instead, explain them as factual. Share your past, then move on to the positive, or discuss the lessons you learned as a result of this experience. A negative can have a positive spin, depending on your outlook. Continue looking toward your aspirations and dreams. Whatever your past, it made you the amazingly resilient, strong person you are now.

<u>Fourth is the Reality Phase:</u> In the reality phase you are seeing each other for who you both truly are, faults and all. He has seen you without makeup, wearing comfortable old clothes, and miraculously, he still finds you attractive. This does not give you the freedom to start wearing comfortable clothes all of the time. The term "letting yourself go" applies to both men and women. Avoid that pitfall by continuing to compliment each other on your appearance, noticing a new haircut or new outfit. These small gestures will encourage your partner to continually look nice for you while you continually look nice for him. My girlfriend still applies fresh lipstick before she goes home from work every evening just to look nice for her husband of 28 years.

Another reality that will present itself during this phase is an illness. Hopefully, it is for a short time, like the flu or stomach bug, and nothing serious. Still, you have to witness the other person during an illness and survive to tell the stories. You will learn quite a bit about your partner when presented with an illness. For example, I like to be left alone when I am not feeling well; however, my partner is the opposite and likes to be taken care of. I will be the first to admit that my partner is a much better caregiver than I am. I know I have to go the extra distance when he is not feeling well.

The best part of this phase is that you start to adjust to your partner. You learn what you need from each other and how best to supply it. Figuring out when to be present and when to give your partner space is an ever-evolving art. Discuss your alone time and how you like to spend it. We all need time to ourselves, some more than others, so carve out how much alone time you both need in advance. Are you comfortable with your partner going on a guy's skiing trip without you? Is he comfortable with your annual sister trip?

You both may be the best communicators in the world, but one thing is guaranteed, you will eventually argue. Navigating and resolving the first full-blown disagreement is a major lesson learned. Disagreements or misunderstandings will creep up again, but you've learned your responses to anger. You've also learned the steps required to defuse the situation. Does your partner withdraw, needing time to analyze things, or does he engage in the conflict immediately? When you are angry at your partner, take a deep breath and do not say anything you may regret. I follow the 24-hour rule, which means biting my tongue for 24 hours and thinking about what I want to say. It is amazing how after this time period, certain things are not as important, or can be phrased in ways that do not attack or accuse. This frees me to present my point of view or communicate what upset me and why. Regardless of individual styles, you both learned how to navigate the path to acceptance and compromise without hurting the one you love.

During this phase, you have also learned each other's dreams. You become a cheerleader, helping to achieve mutual objectives. Encouraging each other to try different things, and pursuing things you may not understand. In summary, you help each other be the best person you can be.

Finally is the Commitment Phase or Partnership Phase: This is where you both decide to enter into a long-term, exclusive relationship for life. You have become best friends and lovers. Your love is a feeling of stability, trust, and shared values. Your shared values will determine your goal for this partnership. For some, that may mean engagement and marriage. If marriage is not your value, it may mean living together or having two different homes while sharing sections of time. Whichever fits you best, you have decided on a future together with no end date.

After you have entered this final phase, remember, and revisit the other phases you have navigated to arrive here. Once arriving at our final destination, we often take the view for granted. You have worked very hard to make it to this phase, so celebrate every day. Relationships are delicate, so handle yours with care.

In addition to a relationship moving through the previouslymentioned four phases, dating through all four seasons is recommended by psychologists and houses of worship. Certain religions will not marry you unless you have been together through all four seasons or one full year, believing you do not fully know a person until you have experienced a year together. There is wisdom in this logic since each season brings new feelings, activities, thoughts, and challenges (not to mention wardrobes).

Melding each other's family obligations,

especially around the holidays, always leads to fascinating discoveries. Many movies have been made from holiday relationship disasters. Hopefully, you can both laugh at your dysfunctional families and accept them for who they are. How boring life would be if we were all the same. Variety is the spice of life!

When you have made it past one year, you have experienced the majority of events once. It is safe to say you have seen each other at your best and your worst. Congratulations on staying together and working through whatever life has thrown your way. This milestone is a monumental achievement not to be taken for granted. Be sure to celebrate it.

During the second year together, when a new challenge arises, you can reflect on the previous year. Was there a similar situation you navigated successfully? Of course, if the situation was dealt with poorly, try a different approach this time around. You will constantly be fine-tuning these points to stay on course. Heraclitus, a Greek philosopher, is quoted as saying, "Change is the only constant in life."

As your journey continues, be sure to keep the love alive. Humans like routine. Routines give us structure, reduce stress, and promote mental, physical, and emotional well-being. However, do not let routines turn you into a boring non-adventurous person. Your first year was filled with new and exciting experiences, a defining part of the attraction; consequently, try not to let your subsequent years become mundane.

When researching reasons for failed long-term relationships or marriages, all reasons can be traced to poor communication. Lack of commitment, constant arguing, infidelity, and unrealistic expectations all stem from a lack of communication. Communication is the most important factor in maintaining a healthy relationship.

Communication was how you started your relationship and how you were able to advance through each phase of your relationship. It only makes sense that it will be how to keep your relationship alive.

Take time to talk to each other every day beyond the regular niceties. Be present when speaking with each other. Do not try to have a serious conversation while watching a television program. Carve out time for each other. A weekly date night for just the two of you helps keep the fires burning. Starting these habits early in your relationship is imperative. Otherwise, spending one-on-one time is easily sidelined. My cousin shared they scheduled weekly sex to keep their love life alive. Every Friday evening was their time to be intimate. That might take scheduling to the next level for some, but it certainly gave them something to look forward to every week.

Another major reason for discord that we have not touched on yet is finances. Money can be the root of all evil: whether it is lack of finances, discrepancy in earning power, how each person spends their money, debt versus savings, or credit score. When first starting to date, you're trying to understand the person's values to see if they align with your own. Pay attention to what he enjoys spending his money on. You do not want to ask about his finances directly, but indirectly you can get a general idea. An indirect question is, "If you won $1 million in the lottery, what would you do?" The answer to this question will help you understand if he likes to save money, spend money, share his money, or a combination of these options. As your relationship continues, you will have a general idea of his income based on his current job or lifestyle.

If college was involved, you can always inquire if he had to take out loans. This topic can easily be worked into the conversation; with the government currently paying off some student loans. Vacations or travel is my favorite topic and can divulge if a person budgets or splurges. These exercises have no right or wrong answers. You are looking for deal-breakers or how to best compromise. For example, if you enjoy high-end restaurants but he does not, this may be your gift when going out for fine dining. If he enjoys concerts, but ticket prices are beyond your comfort level, this may be his gift.

Prior to marriage or a life commitment, it is imperative to disclose all of your finances, including credit card debt, credit score, bank accounts, and most importantly, how you will handle finances individually and as a couple. When people marry at a younger age, they will build their financial nest egg together. Usually entering into a relationship on equal ground. As people get married at a later age, they have already accumulated some wealth or financial independence. Whatever you have accumulated before marriage is not communal property unless you place it in a joint account. Many couples today maintain separate individual accounts, plus a joint account for household expenses. The amount of money each individual enters into the joint account varies from equal amounts to a percentage based on each person's income. This is a conversation each couple needs to agree upon before cohabitation.

Health is another topic that needs full transparency. This is important for all ages. Younger people need to know each other's family history, especially if they are planning on having children. Medical conditions can be genetic, familiar predisposing, or a result of lifestyles. Knowledge of your family medical history allows awareness of what the future may hold for you or your children. Having this knowledge will also allow you to adapt your lifestyle and conduct preventative care. Preventative care includes regular check-ups, screenings, smoking cessation, diet, and exercise. The earlier you identify an issue, the easier it can be to control. If cardiac disease is prevalent in your family, starting a heart-healthy diet and exercise regime can keep you from having a heart attack or stroke. 90% of heart disease is preventable through a healthy lifestyle. If you have a genetic disease in your family, you may wish to consult a genetic counselor before having children. Discussing health issues may not be high on the list for healthy people. This conversation may not come up until you are in the commitment phase, but should still be discussed.

Older couples may already be dealing with health issues and need to have this conversation earlier in the dating process. This should not be a conversation on your first date. I can't think of a quicker way to have your date run for the hills! Whatever the health issue is that you need to discuss, it will guide you toward the right time to reveal this information. Illness is not something to be ashamed of. When discussing a health issue, mention the positive things you are doing for your condition. If your latest lab results were within normal range, then brag a bit, showing you have things under control. If your maintenance includes a specific diet, then help your partner understand your dietary restrictions. You will need your partner's understanding, acceptance, and assistance, especially as time goes by. The goal is to grow old together gracefully.

80% of all chronic illnesses are preventable by addressing the root cause of daily habits. Five areas to address for healthy living are diet, physical activity, stress relief, sleep, and social connection. Learn how to incorporate these into your life; the earlier, the better. Keep each other happy and healthy, go for walks together, learn new recipes, or give each other a back rub. Preserving health is easier than curing a disease.

The question of whether a single person or a married person is healthier has generated many studies with recent conflicting results. Over the past 150 years, it was felt that married individuals were healthier than their single counterparts, with married men showing the greatest improvement. This was credited to married men taking fewer risks, eating better, reducing stress, and enjoying overall better mental health with the support of a spouse. However, more recent studies are challenging this claim. The newer studies are showing married individuals are gaining more weight and exercising less than their single counterparts, again targeting married men as the largest culprits. Singles were credited with having more time to exercise, desiring to keep trim while continuing to date and understanding the need for a healthy diet. Another contributing factor is that there are many different types of relationships today versus traditional marriages. What all studies boil down to is the need for the five areas of healthy lifestyles, regardless if you are single or married.

Work expectations can be a thought-provoking topic. Discuss your career goals, including longevity and advances. If you are looking to start a family, will you both continue to work, or will one person stay home raising the child or children? Stay-at-home-Dads are on an increase from previous years; results indicate one in five non-paying parents were men. Unfortunately, having any parent staying at home full- time is a luxury not afforded by many. At the other end of the spectrum is retirement. If you are counting the days until your retirement, do you have a plan to actively retire? Discuss how you see your later years in life. Without a full work schedule, how will you fill this time? Retirement without a plan to stay active may result in decreased overall health and well-being.

The distribution of household chores will probably be the source of more disagreements. Food shopping, laundry, cooking, washing dishes, house cleaning, and yard work may be fun early in a relationship, but once the novelty wears off, they become just another chore. When surveyed on the division of labor within couples, each person felt they contributed more than their partner. Each person also overestimated their contributions. Try not to fall into this trap. If your partner takes on a chore, simply say thank you. Whatever you do, do not say he did the chore incorrectly. A more accurate statement is he did not do the chore to your standards, but the bottom line is you did not have to do the chore. A word to the wise: do not let him see you "fixing" a chore he just completed. Anyone would wonder why bother taking on a chore if the other person is going to redo it. Be appreciative of each other, and divide the chores according to your strengths and interests.

Finally, pay attention to the topics you disagree on

early in your relationship. Unfortunately, these will be the basis for your future frustrations. People can grow and change but at the core, people will revert to learned behavior. If you are a minimalist and your partner is a collector, you will need to accept this for life. Try to understand the rationale for why your partner has certain habits or behaviors. In this case, the partner who collects items or has difficulty throwing anything away was likely raised in a house with financial constraints. Since he is financially secure now, he values his status by collecting items. This revelation may make it easier for the minimalist to accept his behavior; of course, a storage shed also helps! Compromising is the key to any relationship, so respect and try to understand each other's point of view.

Continuously invest in your relationship to keep the love alive. I had a colleague who was from India and had an arranged marriage. She met her husband for the second time at her wedding. Curiosity had me asking about her feelings regarding an arranged marriage. Would she recommend this for her children? She replied with a thought-provoking statement: "First, I trust my parents to choose a partner for me with the same values and social status. Second, in India, we marry, and then we learn how to love each other. We start with respect, and love grows. In the US, you fall in love first, then marry a respectable time later. However, once you marry, the loving stops." I am afraid she has a point. Once we have our partner, the majority of Americans become complacent, no longer putting in the same effort they previously did while courting. Keeping the romance alive does not need to be difficult. Simple acts or gestures toward each other go a long way. Hold hands or give that extra hug or kiss for no reason. I encourage laughter along with little surprises. A word to the wise: be careful when answering the door wrapped in only Saran Wrap! Maintain your appearance for *your* overall well-being, with the bonus of his appreciation. A nice way to reminisce is by looking at photos of previous vacations or special events and vowing to create future picture-worthy times. Above all else, nourish this person who will always be there for you, remembering why you fell in love with him in the first place. Now that you have found him, never let him go.

Congratulations on finding your Mr. "Not-So" Perfect, who turned out to be Mr. Perfect for you. Imperfections and all. May your journey and love continue to grow.

Conclusion:

I know of one woman who met her husband on her very first online date. My sister met her partner on her fifth online date. Seven out of ten of my nieces and nephews met their matches online. I also know people who have met their significant others, speed dating, parents without partners, and various clubs or outings. As stated earlier, I took a lot longer. I was single for 20 years before meeting my current husband.

In 1997, at the age of 38, I found myself divorced with sole custody of my two beautiful young daughters. I met my first husband when I was 16 years old. We did go our separate ways a few times, the longest being 2 years while I was in college. Still, I had limited dating experience. Imagine my shock when I had to go out into the world and figure out how to date as a single parent.

I tried all of the suggestions on where to meet someone, as mentioned in Step 1. Online dating was a new concept and not socially accepted. Accordingly, the general public viewed online dating with ridicule and skepticism. It was felt that people who used this tool to meet someone were desperate, causing people to hide the fact they met online. A little online history: online dating started with Match.com. in 1995 but did not become popular until 2007, when it became the second-highest online industry. 384 million people worldwide used online dating sites in 2023, including 60 million of these people in the US. Needless to say, online dating is no longer frowned upon by society, and social acceptance has been achieved.

Still, why did it take me so long to find my match? Being a single parent with sole custody and sole financial responsibilities makes you prioritize your circumstances. As a result, working and raising children were a priority over dating. Eventually, I did come around to re-entering the dating world. Next, the challenge was carving out some time for dating. Once this obstacle was overcome, I skeptically started dating again. Something I never thought I would have to do.

My first serious relationship, post-divorce, was with a gentleman who wanted to get remarried. I used to tease that he wanted to get remarried but did not care who the bride was. In this case, there was some truth in that. This particular gentleman did marry the very next person he dated. Men will decide they are ready for marriage and will choose the person best suited around them at that specific time. Women will choose a person and then wait for them to be ready, even if that means waiting for years. For this reason, women should have a time limit on how long they are willing to wait for someone if a commitment is being sought. If you do not set a time limit, you may end up disappointed and re-entering the dating world when the number of single men has declined. After I declined to get re-married, my brother-in-law pointed out that I needed to get dating out of my system since I did not often date when I was younger. He might be right; either way, I felt like I was being pressured to get re-married, so I chose to wait a bit longer before saying, "I do."

I often wonder if it all comes down to timing. The proverbial fork in the road. What if I made a different set of choices, how different would my life be? I put one gentleman in the "friend" category while I pursued the "bad boy." Why do women pursue the bad boy when deep down we know it will not end well? By the time I woke up realizing there was this nice and stable person versus a torturous relationship, this gentleman had met another woman. I missed my opportunity to plead stupidity by two weeks. I am happy to report he is still with this woman, and I wish them both the very best. Was it just not meant to be, or do we create our destiny?

Once my children became teenagers, I decided to put dating on hold. Soon enough, they would be on their own. I would then revisit dating when the girls were out of the house, avoiding the complexities dating with teenage daughters might bring. Besides, I knew I was going to miss them terribly and wanted to spend what little precious time we had together.

Well, we all know that God laughs when you are busy making plans. Once my girls were getting ready to leave their family home, I came down with a very unusual medical condition. I am glad to say after a surgical procedure, I was as good as new. However, this postponed my return to dating another 5 years.

Once I was medically cleared, I decided to relocate from New Jersey to Florida. My girls were on their own, following their dreams. I had learned life was very short and that it was time to follow my dream. The sunshine and the beach were calling me, so I listened and relocated.

I re-established myself in a welcoming new community. When I was not working, I joined various new groups, exposing myself to new activities and experiences. My priority was to make new friends while grasping the dynamics of living in a new area.

Still, a male companion would be nice. So after

my first year, I felt settled and ready to re-enter the dating world once again. I had no intention of re-marrying. I was an independent woman who made a life for myself and was very proud of my achievements.

At the age of 58, I finally met my match. I guess you can say he snuck up on me. I was just looking to have a monogamous relationship where we both maintained our places and had shared time together, nothing more. This person knew just how to handle me. The truth is, he played me like a fine-tuned fiddle. He gave me space when I needed it, and at the same time, let me know he was there. He puts up with my crazy ideas, but will gently tell me when I am being ridiculous. He makes me laugh while encouraging me to stop and smell the flowers. We have common interests, explore new interests, and allow each other to maintain our separate interests. He is the first to include my single girlfriends in things we do, understanding I will always keep my girlfriends. He lets me just be me, as silly as that may sound.

Somehow, he persuaded me to marry him at the age of 60. We chose an April 2020 wedding date, unaware COVID would shut down the entire world on March 17th. This included canceling our original wedding plans. With the help of many people, we regrouped and proceeded with an intimate ceremony. My friend offered her lovely backyard overlooking her pool and marsh as our new venue, while another friend made our wedding cake. My hairdresser snuck me into her house and styled my hair that morning, and our photographer met us for an hour of pre-ceremony pictures with the beach as our background. Our wedding officiant and musician both braved the unknown and joined us in my friend's backyard while a local restaurant catered our delicious meal, including a complimentary bottle of champagne. This wonderful community of people rallied together making our wedding possible.

We were only allowed to gather 10 people in total. Everything was outdoors on a beautiful, sunshiny Florida day. Family and out-of-town guests, including my two daughters, could not attend. Trying to include our family and friends, we learned how to FaceTime, and the entire event was live-streamed to everyone wishing to watch. Even though our group was small, I could feel the love surrounding me. Family and friends were typing comments or sending emojis into the streaming event from afar while my friends played commentator. It was the closest thing to having everyone with me.

This small and intimate ceremony allowed my husband and me to concentrate on ourselves. We did not have to worry about entertaining anyone, nor was there any family drama. It was a pure celebration of our love with a few close friends. We laughed, danced, feasted on a delicious meal, and drank champagne. The evening ended with me in the pool in my wedding gown. Okay, maybe a little too much champagne! I could not have asked for a more perfect wedding day amidst a crazy pandemic. I am still so grateful to everyone who made this possible.

After the ceremony, our family and friends sent us pictures of how they celebrated with us from the comfort of their homes. Various families dressed up in the outfits they originally planned on wearing, gathered celebratory food, danced, and sang right along with us. It turned out to be a positive and shining moment in a period of uncertainty. We turned adversity into good fortune, sharing the love and hope for a bright future.

I am telling you this story to say, never give up. Love can find you at any age. Are things perfect? Of course not. No one is perfect, but right now, things are pretty perfect for me.

As I was writing this book, it dawned on me: to finally meet my match, I used a free dating site, had my first date off-season in January, looked beyond a blurry photo, went outside of my dating radius geographically, plus canceled a second date leaving me to actively pursue another date. If I did not venture outside of my comfort zone on multiple levels, I would still be in the dating world.

I hope that you find some guidance and assistance navigating the dating world in this book. I found the dating world overwhelming and a bit frightening. There were not any reference books for me, so I stumbled my way through these new experiences by trial and error.

A lot has changed with dating over the years. From courtships to free love. Now we have entered the tech world. People today have a lot more freedom to choose the type of relationship they are seeking, including everything from marriage to "friends with benefits". Yet the core of things has remained the same. People are biologically wired to be paired. So go become a pair or partnership.

Best wishes for happiness and success in all that's to come on your journey finding and keeping Mr. "Not-So" Perfect.

Milton Keynes UK
Ingram Content Group UK Ltd.
UKHW041328301124
451950UK00006B/52

9 798330 589654